Echoes of the Ancient World
Series editor Werner Forman

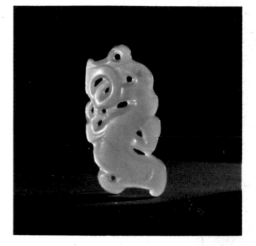

THE MAORI
HEIRS OF TANE

THE MAORI
HEIRS OF TANE

Text by David Lewis
Photographs by Werner Forman
Foreword by D. R. Simmons

ORBIS · LONDON

Dedicated to Jack O'Neill,
killed 1916 in the ranks of the *Hokowhitu a Tu,*
the Battalion of the war god, Tu.

Half-title page:
Two jade ornaments dating from the mid-eighteenth century. Above: A
small taniwha, or monster, found on Banks Peninsula. Below: A marakihau or sea monster
made in the northland. Marakihau often turn into women, and marry men.
When their husbands find out their true natures, they must return to the sea.

Title page:
Front of the storehouse Te Puawai O Te Arawa, carved by Wero of Ngati
Tarawhai for Te Pokiha Taranui of Ngati Whakaue in 1868. This is the last great
storehouse to be built. The central figure represents Tama Te Kapua, captain of the
Arawa canoe from 'Hawaiki' and legendary founder of the tribe.

This page:
Mokau River, linking the interior of the King Country with the Tasman Sea.
The King Country played an important part in the later nineteenth-century resistance of
the Maori to the white man.

© 1982 Orbis Publishing Limited
First published in Great Britain by Orbis Publishing Limited, London 1982

Paperback edition published in 1985
Reprinted 1985

Printed in Yugoslavia by Gorenjski Tisk, Kranj
Hardback ISBN 0-85613-343-4
Paperback ISBN 0-85613-939-4.

CONTENTS

FOREWORD

In the two hundred years that argument has raged about the settlement of the Pacific by Polynesians, many origin theories have been put forward. Yet very few of the people putting forward their views have actually gone to the islands and asked the knowledgeable elders for their opinions. Fewer still, in praising or denigrating the navigational abilities of the Polynesians, have felt it necessary to ask the navigators how they navigated. A non-sailor evaluating the navigational abilities of a people with a totally different culture is an absurdity. A sailor prepared immediately to judge other sailors because they do not do things the same way is equally absurd but much more dangerous.

David Lewis is a small-boat sailor who has been prepared to sail on Pacific canoes with the local navigators and learn. His own yachts have been sailed by Pacific navigators and he has been taught how to navigate in the Pacific manner. In other words, he had the courtesy to ask. The results have astounded the world. In recent times the challenge has been taken up by modern-day navigators and the double canoe *Hokulea* has sailed between Hawaii and Tahiti using only Pacific navigational techniques. Many more such voyages will follow; because even if some Polynesian islands have lost their hereditary navigators, they can regain the lore of their ancestors in David Lewis's *We the Navigators*.

He has now turned his attention to writing a more general book on the land of his birth – New Zealand, better known to its original inhabitants as Aotearoa. The same sensitivity that led David Lewis to ask the navigators to teach him has been applied in this more general survey of New Zealand Maori culture. Necessarily, in writing about Maori life before the *pakeha* (Europeans) came, the past tense is used. But Maori life did not stop with the arrival of Tasman or Captain Cook; it has changed, adapted and taken on new ways but is still just as vigorous as ever. Since the first significant contact, Maori life has gone through many far reaching social changes yet has retained its identity.

In 1769 Maori prehistory was caught alive by Captain James Cook. At the time of his second voyage in 1772, changes had already started to occur in Maori culture. The first and most obvious was the development of trade with Europeans. This entailed an intensification of the local economy to produce cloaks, jade adzes, jade *tiki*, carvings and many other items in return for cloth or iron nails. The second was the competition for access

The Tasman Sea at North Taranaki, on the North Island where canoes crossing the Pacific may have made landfall. Subsequent colonization of both islands took place in repeated waves of settlers moving north to south along the coast.

Above: A nephrite blade which has been partly converted into a heitiki in the early nineteenth century. When nephrite adzes were replaced by imported iron and later by steel, nephrite blades became redundant. But they could easily be converted into saleable heitiki. (Anything in the shape of a human being, whether in greenstone, stone or wood, is a tiki. Heitiki means 'hung tiki' and heitikis were worn by men and women as neck ornaments.)

Right: Kaitaka, a cloak for a man of high rank, with a taniko (tapestry border). The material is made from dressed flax fibre woven by finger-twining into a cloth. This cloak was made in Taranaki, was probably looted during the northern musket raids of the early nineteenth century, and was presented to a missionary.

to the trade areas and supplies of tradeable goods which became apparent on Cook's second voyage. Access to good trading ports became an important factor in demographic changes of the late eighteenth and early nineteenth centuries.

Captain Cook also introduced potatoes to Queen Charlotte Sound. It was almost certainly these potatoes which enabled the agricultural tribes of Canterbury to extend into the previously non-agricultural areas of the extreme south of the South Island. Shortly after Cook's third voyage in 1778, a flourishing trade in dressed flax fibre, timber, potatoes, and later pigs had a very marked effect on Maori life. The potato trade opened up previously inaccessible or marginal areas like Wellington Harbour or the South Island. In the sweet potato growing areas, potatoes replaced the secondary crop yam and, to a certain extent, taro. It lessened the need for seasonal hunting, fishing and fern-root collecting. With its greater yield, the potato allowed the development of a more permanently occupied base village with larger buildings and the time to build them.

The establishment of trading villages on the coast also gave introduced diseases a chance to reach epidemic proportions. The common cold, influenza, measles and many other bacterial or viral diseases were unknown to the Maori. The long isolation of the ancestors in Polynesia and New Zealand with little contact with other peoples, meant that two major epidemics in the late eighteenth or early nineteenth centuries reduced the population, estimated by Cook at 100,000 to 200,000, by about a quarter. Inland tribes either visited or tried to take over good trading areas, thus helping the spread of disease. In the Bay of Islands for example, the tribes seen by Cook in 1769 and who killed Marion du Fresne in 1772 when he stayed too long and posed too much of a threat, were no longer in the area shortly afterwards.

Warfare was an integral and essential part of tribal life. In the early nineteenth century Maori from the Bay of Islands started a series of long-distance raids against the tribes further south. Kororareka was a favoured port for American traders who called in for refreshment after rounding the Horn. They were followed by sealers and later whalers. Some guns were traded to the tribes of that area, who then went on raids down the west coast for more goods, principally flax and flax garments, but soon including a new trade item, dried tattooed heads. No part of New Zealand was left untouched by the raids or by the movement of tribes who wished to get access to good trading areas. As guns became more plentiful, slaughter warfare became common. Pre-European raids appear to have been more like social affairs, with a tribe who had no desire to take over a territory raiding for women, greenstone, a few slaves and a lot of *mana*. There were no projectile weapons used, and fighting was a matter of personal honour and bravery. With guns, the northern tribes dropped the idea of a warrior gaining personal honour from a good fight and concentrated on the goods to be obtained. In twenty years there were thirty major raids south. Fear of such raids became a part of life and whole areas were deserted while the inhabitants withdrew to inaccessible areas. In other areas the people consolidated in strongly fortified villages, but even this was no answer to raiders armed with guns. The chiefs soon learnt not to lead their warriors into battle.

In 1814 English Missionaries settled in the Bay of Islands and introduced hamlet farming centred around the church. A new range of crops including wheat, peaches and apples was introduced, but until 1833 the missions had little success. The reasons are not hard to find. The Bay of Islands tribes up to that period had been the people with guns. Te Rauparaha, one of their allies at Kawhia, had moved his tribe to Wellington and conquered that area, so as to have access to trade and guns. He also wished to control the jade sources of the South Island tribes who had few guns. The South Island groups knew he would be back and took advantage of increasing European trading to obtain guns for themselves. When the northern chief attacked again in 1830, he was met by guns and for the first time the raiders were faced with almost equal firepower. It was the end of raiding and the start of Mission conversion which was also accelerated by despair and the breakdown of tribal life.

In 1840 New Zealand became a British colony after the signing of a treaty with the Maori chiefs. In 1845 war broke out between Maori and European over land. European settlers wanted more land. Some Maori were resisting the sale of their land on principle, other Maori fought with the British on principle.

The war in the North with the chiefs Hone Heke and Kawiti though, had another important aspect. The first fortification built was an improved version of the musket *pa*. The British failed to take it until the defenders had abandoned it, in typical Maori fashion, preferring to keep their force intact rather than undergo a siege. The British used howitzers and cannon. The next *pa* built was improved with underground connecting passages, underground bombproof shelters and traverses on the rifle trench. Five *pa* were built and each one was stronger than the last until the final one, Ruapekapeka, was largely underground and defended by cannon and a captured Congreve rocket. The outer palisades of the *pa* were so strong that a full day of attack by 32 pounders had little effect. Two engineers with the British made plans and models of this *pa* for use at the Imperial Staff College and well they might, as this was the first example of trench warfare the British had ever seen, apart from the other *pa* built for the same war.

Later wars between Maori and European in New Zealand in 1863–8 led to further improvement in trench warfare, until the *pa* had all the features, including underground bunkers, that became necessary in Europe in the First World War with the perfection of the machine gun.

The 1863–8 land wars of European against Maori also saw the development of messianic cults like Pai Marire or Ringatu, Christian religions interpreted in a Maori manner. Almost universally the prophets appealed to the sense of captivity or bondage which their people saw as like that of the Jews in Babylon.

After the land wars the Maori people lived mainly in the rural areas and withdrew from contact with Europeans. The effect of the introduced diseases for those who survived was devastating. Only one family in three had even one child. By 1900 the population was down to 30,000 and politicians were speaking of 'smoothing the pillow of the dying race'. Such was not to be the case. In 1939 with the outbreak of the Second World War there was need for labour in the cities. Many of the Maori people were prepared to leave their retreats and join the *pakeha* in the cities. Maori people are to be found in all professions and trades and are playing a significant and important part in the development of New Zealand. The culture seen by Captain Cook in 1769 has undergone what can only be described as a series of almost complete social revolutions, yet is still strong and vigorous. New and exciting carving is being done for the meeting-houses being built for the *marae*, where the ancient *waiata* or sung poems are still sung to add a relish to the speeches.

D. R. Simmons
Auckland Institute and Museum

TE KORE
The Coming of the Maori

First came Te Kore, the Nothingness. The creation chant lists a genealogy of nine Nothings. Then was Te Po, the Night: Te Po-nui, the Great Night, Te Po-roa, the Long Night; and on and on through measureless ages of darkness until at last came Te Ata – the Dawn. And with the Dawn, out of aeons of Nothings and out of the very womb of darkness itself evolved the primeval parents, Rangi, the Sky Father, and Papa, the Earth Mother. Clasped in each other's arms, Rangi and Papa were happy. They produced children, all sons – in some versions six, in others seventy, the exact number of a traditional war party.

Rangi and Papa were content, but not so their offspring, for with the Sky pressed down upon the Earth they could not share the dawn but stifled in darkness, their only illumination the pale glimmer of the glow-worm. They clung to the side of their Earth Mother, Papa, and sheltered within her armpits. This cramped existence became intolerable. For a long time the sons debated about what should be done.

The wisest of the offspring, Tane-mahuta, father of forests, trees and birds and the god of craftsmen, was for forcibly separating the parents. Whiro, being determined to remain within the body of his mother, led the opposition. There he still abides, the personification of darkness, evil and death, his realm the underworld. Another son, Tawhiri-matea, god of winds and tempests, also disliked Tane's plan. He feared for the integrity of his airy kingdom, should Earth and Sky be torn asunder. He held his formidable breath for a time, but then assailed his brothers mightily, remaining thereafter their implacable enemy.

True to his savage nature, Tu-matauenga, the god of war, was all for killing Papa and Rangi out of hand, but the wise and humane Tane persuaded him not to: 'It is better to rend them apart and to let the Sky stand far above us and the Earth lie below here. Let the Sky become a stranger to us, but let Earth remain close to us as our nursing mother.' And so it was resolved; Tu sided with Tane, and they were joined by three other divine sons, Tangaroa, god of the ocean, Rongo-matane, god of peace and the kumara (sweet potato), and Haumia-tike-tike, god of the fern root. These five proceeded to attempt by turns to accomplish the crucial act whereby the world order as it is at present was to be established.

The peaceful Rongo was the first to try to separate Papa from Rangi, but he did not succeed, and the heavens still lay heavy on the land. Then it was Tangaroa's turn, then Haumia's; they, too, failed. Next the warrior god, Tu, tried his hand. He hacked with might and main at the sinews

Raiatea, Society Islands. Probably 'Hawaiki', legendary homeland of the Maori.

Above: This small steatite female figure is possibly a goddess symbol. It was originally a pendant, and had a pierced lug between the shoulder blades. This type of figure is found only in the northern part of the South Island.

(New Zealand). New Zealand's forests and streams remained virgin – the traditions clearly stated – untrodden by the foot of man, from first creation until the ancestral Maori immigrants stumbled ashore from their storm-battered voyaging canoes.

Whence came these far voyagers? They had sailed from a legendary Hawaiki in tropical Polynesia, a least distance of 2575 kilometres (1600 miles) to the north. With their coming, the peopling of the Pacific basin, which covers a third of the earth's surface, by Polynesian sea rovers was completed.

The story of the Maori really begins at a period when their remote ancestors were strung out along the Indonesian-Melanesian island chain, before they erupted into the insular Pacific. They were not Maori then, nor even Polynesian. They were speakers of the Austronesian group of languages (formerly called Malayo-Polynesian).

Around 5000 BC the Austronesians began an unparalleled seaborne expansion that was to carry them to Viet Nam, the Philippines and Taiwan in the north, to Malaysia and as far as Malagasy (Madagascar) in the west, along the Melanesian islands to the east, and ultimately, the width of the Pacific to Easter Island. Their characteristic watercraft, notably vessels stabilized by outriggers and double (twin-hulled) canoes, that today are called catamarans, remain as mute witnesses to their wanderings across the Indian Ocean and the Pacific Ocean (the twin-hulled canoes belonged only to the Pacific) – more than half way round the world. The motive power of the Austronesian ships was sail. Words for mast, sail, outrigger float, outrigger boom and canoe rollers (only needed for launching very heavy craft) are among the oldest in Austronesian.

By the middle of the second millennium BC some Austronesian sea-roving traders, the Lapita (makers of a characteristic type of pottery, called Lapita ware after the Melanesian village where it was first found), established settlements all along the coasts of Melanesia. They traded their elegantly decorated Lapita pottery and carried obsidian for stone tools well over 1600 kilometres (1000 miles) – from New Britain to Santa Cruz. In their canoes the trader-settlers brought nearly all the useful

Below: Mirror Lake, Fiordland. Fiordland is the name of that area of fiord-like gorges of the mountain range which separates the interior of the South Island from the sea in the west. Surprisingly, this mountain range terminates on both its flanks in fiords, and the fiords dipping into Lake Te Anau and Lake Manapouri are as steep as those which plunge into the Tasman Sea.

plants that were to be introduced into Polynesia – taro, yam, coconut, gourd, paper mulberry, and pandanus. Several mammals came with them too – the pig, the dog and the jungle fowl (the rat was probably a stowaway).

By 1300 BC the Lapita people had pushed out in the teeth of the trade winds across the 640-kilometre-wide Melanesian trench to colonize Fiji. It was probably at this point in time that the double canoe was invented. Tonga was settled by 1200 BC and Samoa soon afterwards. These East Austronesian Lapita people were the first human beings to set foot in Fiji. Tonga and Samoa. In the latter two archipelagos they were spared invasion and, in the course of a millennium of relative isolation, they evolved into the Polynesians. Thus, while the roots of Polynesian culture, language, material resources and marine technology were of ultimate insular Southeast Asian origin, the Polynesians as a race were children of the western Pacific. The Polynesian language seems to have developed primarily in Tonga, though it was in Samoa that the Lapita immigrants

Uninhabited atoll island off the coast of Raiatea ('Hawaiki'), Society Islands.

Far right: This archaic taumata atua, or resting place of a particular god, was found in 1973 on the shores of Akaroa Harbour, Banks Peninsula, after a flood. When a tohunga wished to consult the god, he asked the god to come and rest in his symbol, so he would know the god was present. This godstick is the largest yet found, being over two feet long and weighing over two pounds. It is also one of the oldest ever found. It is made from Manuka wood. It ends in a penis, which suggests that is was a baton, rather than a stick to be put into the ground. The penis-ended baton is well known from Polynesia.

learned to work the characteristic Pacific Island basalt rock into prototype Polynesian adzes. Gradually too, settlement moved inland from the typical Lapita coastal sites, reflecting the development of a more horticultural economy and perhaps the inadequacy of a reef-gathering and inshore fishing economy in face of increasing population.

The Tongan and Samoan Polynesian heartland includes many fertile islands and richly stocked lagoons. By the time of Christ, husbandmen-fishermen had been established there for well over a thousand years, the change from Lapita people to Western Polynesians being signalled by a steady decline in the quantity and quality of pottery and a more land-based way of life. What, then, can have caused sizeable numbers of Samoans suddenly to break away from their tropical paradise to seek a perilous destiny on the unexplored ocean? Population pressures and defeat in war perhaps, or the mysterious birth of an all-compelling restless curiosity? Nobody knows for sure. But whatever the reason, purposive voyagers *did* set forth from Samoa early in the Christian era, and well before the first millennium AD was ended they had colonized the most distant mid-ocean islands, including Hawaii, Easter Island and New Zealand, not one of which had ever before been seen by man. In all the annals of exploration, the world has never known the like.

Newly found islands were time and again christened with familiar names. Savai'i, largest of the Samoas, was singled out as the 'Father-of-all-Islands' by the Tahitian navigator-priest Tupaia, when he described it to Captain Cook. It gave its name, slightly changed, to Havai'i near Tahiti, which was later renamed Raiatea, and which is assumed by some to be 'Hawaiki', the traditional homeland of the New Zealand Maori.

The first major settlement in Eastern Polynesia was in many ways the most remarkable. The men and women of Samoa voyaged in no timorous fashion for, in a short historical period, they straddled almost all Polynesia to arrive in the Marquesas far beyond Tahiti and the Tuamotus, no less than 3200 kilometres (2000 miles) upwind of their starting point. This was no later than AD 300, and possibly some centuries earlier.

It is highly unlikely that this great leap into the unknown was the work of any one generation. In the first place the travellers developed *en route* or acquired, perhaps from the Micronesians to the north, both harpoons

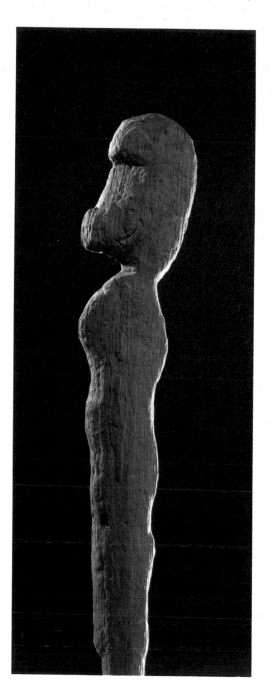

and a new kit of fish-hooks. Secondly, given the wind and current patterns and the sailing ability and endurance of Polynesian craft, the passage was only practicable via various stepping-stone islands.

This same era was marked by a profusion of presumed accidental-drift voyages from Samoa in the opposite direction to the Marquesas, that is with the trade winds to the west, which left inhabitants on dozens of Polynesian outliers in geographical Melanesia. The fact that so many seafarers went astray suggests that this was a voyaging period when many well-provisioned canoes, with crews that included women, were at risk of storms in the course of open sea crossings.

It was not long before the restless discoverers of the Marquesas had found and peopled the major East Polynesian archipelagos. Currently accepted dates are: Easter Island, AD 400, the Society Islands, which include Tahiti, 500, Hawaii, 500 and New Zealand, mainly from the Society Islands with a possible secondary Marquesan influx, between 750 and 1000.

Navigation everywhere in the Pacific was accomplished without instruments, by naked-eye observation and prodigious feats of memory. Guides were (and are) the stars, the sun and the ocean swells, while homing seabirds, clouds and distorted wave-patterns indicated the presence and bearing of land far off. Such methods are surprisingly accurate.

Pacific settlement is known to have resulted from an amalgam of deliberate voyages and accidental drifts. The main stream of colonization was from west to east, from the Asiatic towards the American side, and against the prevailing winds and currents. Computer studies have demonstrated the high probability of east to west drifts with the wind (indeed many hundreds are documented). But long west to east passages like that from Tonga – Samoa to the Marquesas – Tahiti, and north-south ones like those from Hawaii to New Zealand were absolutely barred to drifters by the configuration of currents and winds. These could only have yielded to deliberately navigated probes up or across wind.

This does not mean that successful explorers necessarily returned home, although the orientation ability of trained navigators was fully adequate. Still less does it imply that the discovery of new land, no matter how diligently the explorer has cast about, can be other than fortuitous. The seeker may suspect its presence from drifting branches and the like and keep on in the likely direction but, until he finds land, he cannot *know* that it is there.

The Tahitians or Cook Islanders (there is evidence which suggests that at this time the Cook and Society Islands were, in fact, one cultural unit) could not have known that New Zealand lay over the horizon to the south west (although they might well have inferred it from the flight path of the migrating shining cuckoo), unless some bold and lucky mariner had happened upon New Zealand and returned to tell the tale. There are Ngapuhi legends, it is true, describing such a discoverer, called Kupe, but there is no real evidence for a historic Kupe.

What of the actual vehicles of migration, the Polynesian sea-going ships? The word 'canoe' is rather a misnomer for *pahi*, the double-hulled sailing vessels some of which were longer than Captain Cook's *Endeavour*, though most were smaller, generally about 18 metres (60 feet) long. They were V-sectioned and built of wide planks or strakes, sewn together with sennet and caulked with breadfruit sap and coconut fibre. Ribs were inserted to stiffen the hulls. The sails were of matting. The great Tahitian *pahi* and their Tongan counterparts were noteworthy examples of types of voyaging canoe. Both were, in Cook's words, 'fit for distant navigation'.

Apart altogether from these long-distance catamarans, the Polynesians

Left: Marae (heiau) at Honaunau on the west coast of Hawaii.

Right: This pre-European-contact war-canoe stern post (taurapa) from Waikanae, near Wellington, has suffered greatly from weathering, and has lost all its surrounding scroll-work, so that only the spine and the figure remain.

constructed according to circumstances any of a whole gamut of Austronesian watercraft – outriggers, dugouts and rafts. Not surprisingly, the capacious, seaworthy but clumsy *pahi* that may have voyaged to New Zealand were unsuitable for coastal work and fishing, as indeed, they had been in the Tahitian and Cook Islands groups. Double canoes were retained in New Zealand mainly for use in the stormy waters round Stewart Island, and some were still in the Bay of Plenty as recently as 1769, but generally, single-hulled paddling canoes had replaced them. Sail became merely an auxiliary means of propulsion, though one of the basic Austronesian sail types was retained, a mastless triangular sail, point down, that was also the rig of Samoan outriggers and can be seen on fishing sampans off Jakarta today. Huge trees favoured the construction of dugouts. They were easier to build (with stone tools) than planked craft and were stronger and more durable – at the price of buoyancy and seaworthiness.

One point is all too readily forgotten, especially when the magnificence of Tahitian war fleets or the perfection of Maori war canoes is considered – these ships were constructed entirely without metal tools. Basalt adzes, shell-tipped drills and endless patience built them; they were exclusively the products of the Stone Age.

The circumstances of the settlement of New Zealand have been for years the subject of lively debate, with the upshot that certain long-accepted notions have had to be abandoned. The development of Maori culture is now revealed to have been a continuum within New Zealand, but many questions remain to be answered.

First of all there is the question of tradition. The Maori told Sir Joseph Banks, chief scientist of the *Endeavor* on Cook's first visit in 1769, that their homeland was called Hawaiki, and that it lay to the north of New Zealand in an area of many islands. Unfortunately no one else seems to have enquired into Maori origins for the next three quarters of a century, by which time Maori seamen had sailed on European ships the length and breadth of the Pacific, so unwittingly 'contaminating' their traditions.

From the 1840s onwards tribal ancestral lore was collected. The most common form of the story ran like this: Kupe discovered New Zealand in AD 925 (a date of enviable precision). There were no inhabitants. He returned to Hawaiki (Raiatea) from Hokianga (*Hokianga Nui a Kupe*, the Great Returning Place of Kupe).

A Melanesian-Polynesian people, the *Tangata Whenua*, the People of the Land, settled New Zealand from Western Polynesia at some indeterminate date. They were also called Moriori, a name now reserved for the Maori settlers who colonized the Chatham Islands from New Zealand.

Toi and Whatonga, the legendary explorers, brought the first Polynesian settlers to New Zealand from Hawaiki around 1125.

Around 1350, a fleet of named canoes, each ancestral to a Maori tribe, arrived from Hawaiki. The most important canoes were *Tainui, Te Arawa, Aotea, Tokomaru, Takitimu, Kurahaupo* and *Matatua*, all names of major significance in Maori tribal tradition.

The picture revealed by archaeology is more prosaic. Initial settlement took place between AD 750 and 1000, which fits in well enough with the early tenth century date for Kupe. The settlers brought an undifferentiated eastern Polynesian culture, most probably from the Tahiti area. This period is now known as the Moa Hunter or Archaic phase of New Zealand culture. This developed, without significant outside influence, into the Classic Maori culture from about 1300 onwards. The '*Tangata Whenua*' were simply Polynesian Moa Hunters. New Zealand may well have been settled by several groups at different times. However, such immigrants, especially any later ones, would not have materially affected the culture of fully established communities.

As to the fleet traditions, it is now accepted that they may represent internal migration within New Zealand associated with the revolutionary agricultural and social changes of the fourteenth century that ushered in the Classic Maori culture. Once again, the dates tally with tradition.

One intriguing question remains. Were all the colonizers of New Zealand one-way voyagers who could not have known the land existed, or did some return to tropical Polynesia bearing sailing directions for the new southern land? The most sketchy directions would have been adequate for such a huge target as New Zealand. A return voyage, on the other hand, would culminate in groups of small islands. But it was (and is) customary for Pacific Island navigators to aim deliberately into the middle of archipelagos and subsequently follow 'land signs' to the nearest island. In terms of wind patterns, food supplies for a lengthy voyage and ease of landfall, the return from New Zealand to eastern Polynesia would have been a difficult undertaking, but it would have been far from impossible in terms of the sailing qualities of *pahi* and known Polynesian navigational skills. Whether such voyages ever were made is not known as yet. It is highly probable that they were.

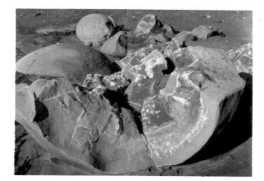

FROM MOA HUNTER TO CLASSIC MAORI

The Polynesians and their forebears right back to the original Austronesian-speaking Indonesian stock were tropical beings. Those of the Polynesians who settled New Zealand were the first of their race ever to encounter a temperate environment. There was nothing in their experience to prepare them for the shocking phenomenon of frost, that destroyed in one season the precious breadfruit saplings, banana shoots and seed coconuts they had jealously nurtured through more than a month at sea. That the immigrants survived at all, much less developed in time a prosperous economy and a rich culture, is a tribute to their extraordinary adaptability and resilience.

The Maori colonizers of New Zealand arrived roughly around AD 800, and they came from tropical Eastern Polynesia; this much is known. But whether there was one migration or several, and whence in Eastern Polynesia the colonists originated is debatable, for adzes, pendant ornaments, harpoon heads, fish-hooks and the like were virtually identical throughout the whole area at this period.

The Maori newcomers to New Zealand lost no time in occupying coastal sites in both the North and South Islands, exploiting the virgin resources of coast and bush – shellfish, fish, berries, birds. Hunting and gathering were not difficult because, since the dawn of creation, New Zealand had been innocent of man.

Subsequent Maori history was largely determined by the suitability for agriculture of the different climate regions. These were three in number: Iwitini (Many Tribes), the fertile northland least prone to frost; Waenganui (Transitional), which was marginal to kumara cultivation; the Wahi Pounamu (the Place of the Greenstone), which remained forever outside the agricultural pale.

It was high summer, according to legend, with the pohutukawa trees blazing scarlet all along the North Auckland coast, when these first human beings came to the silent land. Of their animals, only the *kuri* (dog) and the stowaway rat survived the crossing of the Great Ocean of Kiwa, which proved too much for the Polynesian chicken and the pig. Breadfruit and coconut could not establish themselves. Taro, yam, gourd and *aute* (the paper mulberry whose bark was used for clothing) found a precarious foothold, but only just. Another plant, the kumara, which had been transported from South America, also survived on a few sunny river flats in the far north, and this was the plant which was ultimately to transform New Zealand's economy and culture.

Skull and neck of a moa, mummified in the dry atmosphere of a Central Otago cave.

But the kumara agrarian revolution was still centuries in the future. The first comers found Aotearoa – The Land of the Long White Cloud – to be abundantly stocked with berries, stringy but nourishing bracken roots, and birds of swamp and forest. There were seals and dolphins to be harpooned, shellfish to be gathered at low tide and eels to be trapped in weirs, in the estuaries. As coastal canoe people, they led an idyllic, semi-nomadic life in response to the cycles of natural resources. These were peaceful people. Few in number, they must, at first, have lived very well on the bounty of land and sea. There was no warfare and hence no weapons nor fortified hill-top villages in that early golden age.

In the vast forests of the South Island lived that giant, flightless bird, the moa, whose early abundance has led some anthropologists to call the Archaic Maori the 'Moa Hunters'. But climatic changes, in process since the close of the last ice age 11,000 years before, were at work to destroy the moa. The cool conditions that had prevailed during the ice age favoured the growth of *podocarp* (rain) forests, and it was on the fringes of rain forest and savannah, where seeds and berries were abundant, that the twenty species of moa thrived. The largest, *dinornis maximus*, was three metres (10 feet) tall. Then broadleaf and beech trees began competing with the podocarps, stifling their natural regeneration beneath heavy shade. Gradually, the rain forest was squeezed back into the mountains, maintaining elsewhere but a precarious foothold.

By far the greatest concentration of moa lived on the eastern plains of the South Island, in a mixture of rain forest and grassland. Here, too, flourished the bulk of the Archaic Maori population. And it was the Maori who tipped the already delicate ecological balance – against the rain forest and against the moa. The forests, which were already beginning to die, and their important inhabitants, the moa, finally succumbed to fire, used by the Maori as an aid to hunting. Fire has always been a major weapon of the hunter. In the brief span of 250 years, between 1100 and 1350, the destruction of the trees that still clothed the plains of Canterbury and Otago was finished off by the Maori Hunters. The tussock grasslands, with their scattered stands of beech, that replaced the burned forest, made a poor environment, unproductive of seeds and berries. The moa population plummeted, and by the seventeenth century it was extinct; the concentration of the hunters declined as well. Deprived of their main food supply, the Maori evacuated the South Island inland areas and moved back to the coast. Thus, as men have always done, the Maori showed an uncanny ability to single out and kill the goose that lays the golden egg.

Eventually the hand of man, which had been too heavy for the ecologically fragile rain forest and its flightless birds, gradually depleted the resources of the sea and shoreline. The South Island population declined. On the North Island, an identical Archaic Eastern Polynesian culture still prevailed, but it was from there that the winds of change would ultimately blow.

Mount Carmel was a prehistoric settlement at a harbour mouth in the extreme north of New Zealand that was occupied from 1150 to 1260 by hunter-fishermen. Striking evidence of the mobility of these people is provided by the fact that all the fifty-seven adzes which were unearthed there had been made from basalt quarried at Tahanga on the Coromandel Peninsula some 320 kilometres (200 miles) away. As on the South Island, no weapons were found, nor was there evidence of cannibalism.

An important clue to the way of life of the Archaic Maori can be found in their adzes, and much can be learned about their transition from coastal dwellers to farmers from the radical changes in this essential tool.

Above left: This rock drawing may represent a moa chick in embryo. Negative composition of space (creating a design as much in the negative, unfilled spaces as in the positive, filled spaces) is common in Maori art, and prominent in rock drawings.

Below left: Painted war-canoe paddle, collected by Captain Cook on the East Coast of the North Island in 1769. Unlike Polynesian paddles, Maori paddles have a long, flat blade. The wood's natural surface has been used to make the pattern, while the background has been coloured with red ochre mixed with shark oil.

Below: Sea birds and seal colony of the Kaikoura Peninsula, South Island.

At the beginning of New Zealand prehistory only one design of adze and one kind of rock were being used. These were of the generalized eastern Polynesian type, and remained in use in New Zealand throughout the Archaic period.

The early adzes were made of close-grained basalt or argillite-type rock, as were those of tropical Polynesia. They had a low angle of attack, and a curved cutting edge so that the blade bit into the wood at an angle of about 20 degrees in a slicing, gauging stroke. An angled butt prevented the lashings that held the blade to the wooden haft from being scraped. These were clearly instruments designed to slice out long slivers of wood, to gouge out grooves, but they were quite unsuitable as chopping tools. These early models, which have recently been unearthed in peaty swamps, were instruments *par excellence* for the delicate shaping of dugout hulls, carved wash-strakes, bow and stern pieces and outrigger attachments.

The later adzes of the Classic Maori period were of coarse-grained gabro or sandstone-greywacke. They were evenly bevilled for chopping or splitting. Heavy wood-working adzes (or axes, depending on the mode of hafting used), their tough, coarse raw material could sustain the heavy impacts of forest clearing, grubbing up massive roots without causing damage.

Right: Ferns in the fertile rain forest, south of MacKinnon Pass, Fiordland.

Below: A hinaki, or eel trap, twined from vine. It was made in the Tuhoe area of the central part of the North Island in the mid-nineteenth century.

Top: A rock drawing of a bird from Maerewhenua shelter on a tributary of the Waitaki River in the South Island. Investigators have suggested that this drawing represents a hovering eagle. The eagle, like the moa, has been extinct in New Zealand for over 400 years. It was occasionally hunted by the early Polynesian settlers of New Zealand.

Above: An archaic Maori rock drawing of two men poling a mokihi, a raft canoe made from rushes. This drawing is in the Hazelburn limestone shelter on the Opihi River, South Canterbury, and probably dates to about 1400. Mokihi were still in use well into the nineteenth century for bird-hunting on lakes and for running rapids.

The reasons for the changes are obvious. The development of Classic Maori agriculture demanded powerful tools for forest clearance, for shaping heavy timbers for fortifications and for digging kumara storage pits in hard ground. The later Maori did not, of course, lack canoes, but their function, relative importance and design altered radically. Big, double-hulled, long-distance sailing craft were out of place in this new world. They gave way to craft that were generally single-hulled and paddled and were better adapted to the coastal and estuarine tasks they had to perform.

The pre-European-contact Maori had a very thorough knowledge of the properties of stone. In Stone Age cultures stone was the very stuff of life. Stone tools were needed to make canoes, houses, spears, bird-snares, harpoons, digging-sticks, fish-hooks, nose flutes, carvings and virtually all else that supported and enriched the life of man. It is unlikely that many people today possess nearly such thorough knowledge of the properties of stone or skill at working it as had been mastered by the 'simple' prehistoric Maori.

The Archaic phase did not suddenly give way to the Classic phase in one dramatic transformation. The processes of change, that started in the north, were irregular in space and time. In fact, in Te Wahi Pounamu, the southern region where kumara would not grow, many aspects of the old way of life continued right up to the time of European contact. Perhaps the best way to reconstruct a picture, though somewhat distorted by the passage of time, is to look at the early nineteenth-century way of life of the People of the Greenstone.

Although the southern Maori were by this time cultivating the frost-resistant European potato, they had by no means abandoned their traditional, naturally occurring food resources, nor gone over to year-round permanency of settlement. Bushbirds, groundbirds, eels, shellfish, seabirds and seals, found in their particular settings and seasons along the coasts or in the interior, were still important in the diet.

This, for instance, was the seasonal cycle of the Ruapuke Islanders, whose inhospitable home lies in the stormy Foveaux Strait between Stewart and South Island. January and February (the southern summer) they spent at home, harvesting potatoes and making kelp bags as containers for preserved muttonbirds (*titi*). In March they sailed to the Muttonbird Islands off Stewart Island, remaining there until May, when they returned to Ruapuke with their haul. In June they crossed to the South Island mainland to hunt wood hen (*weka*). In August they moved further inland into the forests after bushbirds. September found them making their way up the Mataura River to Tuturau to gather lampreys. Eeling activities were extended to coastal areas in November. Finally, in December, the Islanders recrossed Foveaux Strait and returned to Ruapuke.

This southland of New Zealand and the Chatham Islands, which retained Archaic features, can offer a few more pointers to the life and the artifacts of the tropical-bred eastern Polynesians, who showed their mettle in face of snow and savage storm. Versions of every type of Polynesian watercraft were still being made and used along those inhospitable shores in the early nineteenth century. There were simple dugouts, five-part canoes (with built up sides and added end pieces), outrigger canoes, double canoes and *raupo* (bulrush) reed raft-boats with raised sides and ends, called *mokihi*. Each type of craft was used for the purpose and in the place for which it was best adapted – the *mokihi*, for instance, being constructed near and used on inland lakes and rivers.

Pathetically few carvings and other art objects which date from the Archaic Moa Hunter period now remain, but enough have survived to show that this was a highly gifted and artistic people. Broken-toothed rectangular combs, a famous dog amulet from Canterbury, the splendid pair of whale-ivory pendants from Kaikoura river mouth, an equally famous ridge-pole carving preserved in a swamp in Kaitaia – and not very much more.

There is, however, one particular art form, rock art, which is virtually confined to the Archaic period and to limestone areas of inland Canterbury and Otago. With the burning of the forests and the decline of the moa, these regions were abandoned, and by the fourteenth century all the inhabitants had trekked off down to the coast. About 350 galleries of drawings, in red and black and done with dry pigments, were left, mainly on cliffs, overhangs and rock shelters – never in deep caves. Realistic representations of human beings, moa, forest birds, dogs and fish are common subjects. There are also 'bird man' figures and the splendid monsters, so favoured by later Maori wood-carvers, called *taniwha*. Both *taniwha* and 'bird man' motifs are well represented in eastern Polynesia, especially in Hawaii and Easter Island.

The fragile nucleus of cultivation that survived precariously in the far north of New Zealand proved to be the vital seed from which the Classic Maori economy was to derive. The original Eastern Polynesian settlers had been practised agriculturalists. But the immediate spread of cultivation in the new land was inhibited by the fact that virgin natural resources were so plentiful, and was also deterred by the devastating effects of frost.

The problem of frost was eventually overcome by the invention of sophisticated systems of warmed and insulated storage-pits to protect the kumara crop, and especially the seed tubers, from freezing. This complicated technology could only have been worked out over a lengthy

A pair of chevron pendants made of whale ivory, from Kaikoura, north-eastern South Island. Here the archaic phase persisted until the late eighteenth century.

Above: This model war canoe was made by a Gisborne carver in the mid-nineteenth century. The war canoe was the proudest possession of a hapu (clan) in the eighteenth century. In the early to mid-nineteenth century, the carved storehouse took over this role. Later, ceremonial meeting houses replaced storehouses.

Below: This large nephrite adze from Claudelands, Waikato, was probably used for tree-felling and for ceremonials as well. Nephrite is harder than steel.

period of trial and error, for there was no tropical experience to draw upon. Ten-metre-wide storage-pits were covered with layers of soil to insulate their contents and maintain a constant temperature. Fires were lit annually in the pits to destroy fungi and pests. The tubers needed special treatment before planting to ensure sprouting. Shallow, fire-warmed pits were hollowed out and lined with alternate layers of dried fern and tubers. They were covered with earth and left for three weeks before the tubers were removed from their hot beds and carefully planted in previously loosened soil that had been lightened by the addition of sand and ash.

The native bracken root increased in importance as a follow-up semi-crop after the kumara had been harvested. Fern rhizomes from dug-over and charcoal-fertilized land were found to be larger and richer in starch than wild ones, so the humble semi-cultivated fern root became a staple of New Zealand diet, rivalling the kumara.

Once the original natural resources of the land had been depleted, the spread of agriculture was, of course, a necessity. South of Christchurch, the absolute outer limit for kumara cultivation, there was no option except depopulation. In the warmer northern regions, on the other hand, there *was* an option. Kumara and fern root fuelled an enormous increase in population – an increase that was to have revolutionary consequences. The process began in the climatically favoured Northland. The rich volcanic soils of the Auckland isthmus were being broken by digging sticks. Soils were artificially enriched when necessary. In the environs of Auckland there remain traces of field boundaries and drainage ditches in the shadow of a terraced *pa* (fortified hill) carbon-dated to 1300.

Between about 1300 and 1500 the new way of life spread throughout Iwitini and more slowly through the blustery Waenganui, leaving indelible imprints in the form of kumara storage-pits, *pa*, new types of adzes, houses, ornaments and weapons.

Heavily armed northerners, their numbers sustained by their agricultural economy, swept southward overland and along the coast in their great canoes to Taranaki and the Bay of Plenty. The canoes *Tainui* and *Te Arawa* seem to have been the first. The others, *Aotea, Tokomaru, Takitimu, Kurahaupo* and *Matatua* followed at various times during the course of the fifteenth century.

The newcomers from northern Auckland fell upon the coast-dwelling Maori hunter-gatherers, who were the *Tangata Whenua* – the original occupiers of the land. The peaceful and outnumbered *Tangata Whenua* were slaughtered or enslaved. The survivors, their cultural heritage largely extinguished, were ultimately absorbed into the tribes of the fierce invaders. Not only did the enslaved provide a labour force for forest clearing and fort building, they also constituted a supplement to the supply of protein food, which had been deficient since the moa had vanished. Thus was the era of cannibalism ushered in. Many scholars believe, however, that the Maori did not eat human beings for their food value, but rather to humiliate the corpses, or those who survived them. It is also possible that the flesh of the distinguished dead was seen as imparting a kind of power to those who partook of it. This idea seems to be borne out by the fact that women in most tribes were not allowed to eat this meat.

It is easy to oversimplify the development of agriculture. For instance, a well-developed horticultural system flourished near Wellington at the astonishingly early period of 1100 to 1400 when, by rights, there should have been no significant cultivation in New Zealand at all – much less in inclement Waenganui.

This gallant early experiment was eventually abandoned but, despite all setbacks, the new culture did finally triumph. By the eighteenth century, even the non-agricultural parts of the South Island had been brought within its orbit. The export of greenstone to the north was a peaceful activity; the spread of weapons, *pa* and warfare was most decidedly not.

The Classic Maori era produced magnificent wood carvings, bone and shell ornaments, decorated clothing and profoundly moving songs and chants. All these were the products of an artistically gifted population, probably numbering no more than 100,000 to 150,000 which was, moreover, divided into some forty warring tribes. Not only were their material achievements impressive, but their intellectual and spiritual life, with associated beliefs and ceremonials, was rich and elaborate.

Rain forest, south of MacKinnon Pass, Fiordland.

TE KAUAE RUNGA

Things Spiritual

It was not uncommon for Maori elders to be able to recite their genealogies back for twenty or more generations, for theirs was a society based on kinship and seniority of descent. It was but fitting that the spirit world should be ordered in like manner. Thus, though Rangi, the Sky Father, and Papa, the Earth Mother, were the primordial parents, they themselves were descended from a long line of personifications of the ultimate, of Nothingnesses and of Nights. From the high gods who were the children of Rangi and Papa, especially from Tane and Tangaroa, were descended the beings of the world below, trees and birds, men and women, even winds and waves. All possessed the living spirit and all were kin to one another – and by no means immune to fratricidal strife. The great Maori scholar-soldier Sir Peter Buck (Te Rangi Hiroa) comments rather dryly that the recitation of spiritual lineages not only made order out of chaos in the spiritual sense, but also had the practical effect of 'giving added length and prestige to the human line of descent', thus enhancing the *mana* (spiritual power) of the chieftain whose ancestry was being extolled by the orator.

The most important of the gods was Tane. He was father of trees and birds, of all the things of the forest, besides being the god of craftsmen, shipwrights, carpenters and wood carvers. He was the maker of woman and the progenitor of man. But here a word of caution. Particular tribes and individual sages held different versions of the 'gospels'. For instance, in some accounts, Tu rather than Tane represents unborn man, and there are different versions of many myths.

Nevertheless, there were some beliefs that were universal throughout Polynesia as well as New Zealand. For instance, no tree must be felled without an invocation to obtain Tane's blessing and without an offering. Failure to do so incurred divine anger. So it was that, when a man named Rata felled a tree without having obtained sanction, the woodland spirits promptly re-erected it. When Rata chided them for having undone his work, they replied: 'Who gave you permission to fell Tane to the ground?' Rata was deeply shamed and admitted his error, at which the spirit servants of Tane forgave him and even went so far as to complete the canoe for him.

Buck gives an example of the completed canoe being regarded as the personification of Tane in the following lines which he quotes from the chant of *Aotea* canoe:

Between Lake Manapouri and Lake Te Anau, in the heart of the Fiordland. A hiatus between rains.

33

Sacred the road
Of Tane struggling below
Of Tane struggling with heaven

(from Sir P. Buck, *The Coming of the Maori*)

Here Tane represents the *Aotea* canoe striving against the ocean waves below and against the storm winds driving from the sky above.

Bird-hunters in the forests recognized Tane as the lord of their quarry, and the first bird killed was laid aside with appropriate prayers as an offering to the god. The rest belonged to the fowlers.

When the time came for men to leave this world it was along the *Ara Whanui a Tane,* the Broad Road of Tane, that stretched westward over the realm of Hine-moana, the Ocean Maid, that they passed. And on this ultimate journey it was Tane-te-Waiora, Tane the Shining One, who guided their footsteps down the golden path of the setting sun.

For the old-time Polynesian sea-rovers Tangaroa, god of the ocean, was probably next to Tane in eminence. But in classical New Zealand, that world of stockaded fort and stealthy ambush, it was Tu, the killer and eater of men, who was most revered. Tu has not been quite forgotten in modern times. Was not the name of the so-called Maori Battalion, that fought with such distinction in both World Wars, actually *Te Hoko-whitu a Tu*, 'the War Party dedicated to Tu'?

But even the terrible Tu had his limitations. While opposing Christian nations have customarily invoked one and the same God of Hosts against each other and seen nothing contradictory in the proceeding, the Maori were more perceptive. In conditions of actual combat, tribal war gods were preferable since they could be relied upon to stand by their own. A tribe must have its own god, the Maori reasoned, because a god common to all 'might be giving ear to the prayer of someone else'. But if a tribal god's loyalty was beyond doubt, his power was another matter. When the Ngapuhi were attacking the Arawa on an island in Lake Rotorua, the Arawa dipped in the lake a lock of human hair braided with bark, which was the symbol of their god Ihungaru, to provoke a tempest against the invading canoes. Unhappily for the Arawa, the Ngapuhi god proved the stronger and the assault succeeded.

Maori religion was essentially animistic. Not only the living beings, but all natural phenomena were personified, and all were possessed of souls or spirits, or *mauri*. This word *mauri* is often translated as 'soul', but 'active life principle' might be more precise, because a creature's *mauri* ceased to exist at the death of the body. It could not leave the body at death and go into the spirit world as did the true soul, *wairua*.

Everything possessed *mauri* – the sky, sun, moon, stars, seasons, wind, rain, mist, night, day, trees, stones, animals, man. Natural forces were frequently personified as Hine (Maid). Thus Hine-te-uira represented the lightning, Hine-rau-wharangi the growth of plants, Hine-whaitiri the thunder, Hine-ahiahi the evening, and so on. Sometimes a legendary ancestor was personified in this manner, like Uenuku, a famous character from Hawaiki, who came to be identified with the rainbow.

It would be an oversimplification to suppose that an object's *mauri* necessarily always dwelt within it. The material *mauri* of a river, for instance, was often a stone concealed somewhere near the source after it had been sanctified by ritual. Its presence would ensure an abundance of fish and waterfowl. Should the talisman be discovered and removed by ill-disposed people, the fish and birds of the river would move elsewhere. The Whanganui people did not place the stone *mauri* of an eel-weir at the weir itself, but concealed it near a waterfall. This was to frustrate anyone who might seek to deprive the *mauri* of its *mana,* or spiritual power, by means of magic spells, since the *mauri* would be unable to hear the spells because of the noise of the cataract.

The stone used as *mauri* of a *pa,* or fortified settlement, was often buried at the base of the first stockade post erected. It was not in itself the guardian of the village, but was merely a *taumata atua,* an abiding place or shrine for the gods, who were the true guardians.

Though stones were very often consecrated as *mauri,* such an identification was by no means invariable. The sea *mauri* of the Whanau-a-Apanui Tribe, for instance, was a rata tree. The first fish caught in any season was deposited at the tree as an offering to the gods.

The symbols of the gods, or *atua,* were many and various but, as with the *mauri* that guarded a fort, the symbols only represented the *atua,* they were not the gods themselves. The symbols or manifestations of the gods could be rainbows, lightning, comets, thunder or earthquake, or equally, a particular tree or rock. There were also material symbols of the gods which were named *toko.* These were often peg-shaped wooden figures that were stuck in the ground during kumara planting, divination and other highly *tapu* (sacred) activities. *Toko* were painted with the sacred red ochre and had ornamental bindings, whose patterns were highly significant. Interestingly enough, though the human form abounds in Maori carvings on houses, canoes, village gateways and memorials to the dead, those particular carvings may represent ancestral figures, but never gods.

Stone images could represent gods, especially Rongo, and were generally placed round kumara plantations. Invariably they were roughly finished and never art objects. In no sense were the images considered to *be* gods, they were merely *taumata atua,* resting places of the gods.

As mentioned earlier, the great Tane breathed life into Hine-ahuone,

Opposite: An epa, or front wall slab for a storehouse which stood in Waitara in North Taranaki. It portrays two female figures entwined, the leg of the top figure going through the eyebrow of the lower one. The carving was done with stone tools in the late eighteenth or early nineteenth century.

Below: Rangitikei River estuary, west coast of the North Island.

the maid he had formed out of the red earth, and they had a daughter, Hine-titama, the Dawn Maid, whom Tane also took to wife. Hine-titama became the mother of mankind. But human life, *ira tangata*, unlike *ira atua*, the existence of gods, involved mortality. How was it that this inexorable destiny of death came into the world? Here is the story.

Tane and the Dawn Maid had a daughter, whom they named Hine-rau-wharangi, the personification of the growth of plants. She was the first infant to be baptized after the Maori ritual, in which a little bird called *miromiro* was liberated to become a link between the child and the gods.

But it was at that time that an irreconcilable role conflict arose between Hine-titama and Tane.

'Who is my father?' Hine-titama asked her husband.

Tane evaded her question, replying obliquely, 'Ask the posts of our house; they will tell you.'

Realizing from this that Tane himself must be her father, Hine said, 'I will go down into the Underworld, into the body of our ancient Earth Mother. There I will prepare a place for our descendants.'

Then Hine fled towards Poutererangi, where commences the path that leads down to the Underworld and, pausing at the portal, she looked back and called out to the weeping Tane who was following her, 'Go back, Tane, rear our children and bring them into the world of life. I will draw them down into the Underworld and protect their spiritual welfare.' So saying, she turned and, passing through the gateway, hurried down into the subterranean darkness, where she assumed the name of Hine-nui-te-po, Great Lady of the Darkness. Although she became the goddess of death, she remained a kindly deity, who cared for the descendents of Tane when their time came to join her in the Underworld.

In tales like this, the Maori myth-makers reveal a genius for explaining the essential unity of the great opposing principles that make up the cosmos. Spiritual and temporal, male and female, life and death, all ultimately derived from the eternal contrast between sky and earth. As Schwimmer points out in *The World of the Maori*, these contrasting sets of principles have nothing in common with the Judaeo-Christian concept of evil being opposed to good. Rather, they are necessary parts of a single harmonious creation.

The demi-god Maui was the outstanding culture hero of the Maori and, indeed, of all Polynesia up to and including the distant Micronesian islands hard by Asia. Rather surprisingly, this universally known character, who had at his disposal potent magic, was never worshipped as a god except in Tonga. He belongs to the group of mythological beings whom the anthropologist, Claude Lévi-Strauss, terms 'mediators', ambiguous characters who move between polar opposites like heaven and earth, gods and men. It was because Maui fished up the Polynesian lands out of the ocean, slowed the sun's daylight passage, brought fire to man and attempted to conquer death that he was known as the great mediator on mankind's behalf – albeit a very tricky one.

Maui was not born in the usual way. His mother miscarried of him by the seashore and, wrapping the foetus in a tuft of her topknot (*tikitiki*), consigned him to the waves. He was rescued from the seaweed by his great ancestor, Tama-nui-ki-te-rangi, who reared him until he returned to his parents. Maui, who is sometimes called Maui-tikitiki, was the youngest of five brothers. According to Maori belief, embryos become mischievous spirits and Maui's escapades fully confirmed the expectation. He tricked his old grandmother out of her magic jaw-bone and performed all manner of marvels with its aid.

Opposite: Bowen Falls plunging into Milford Sound.

Above: Figure above the door of a storehouse which stood in the East Cape area in the early nineteenth century. It symbolizes the gate to the Underworld. To enter it was to die unless tapu was lifted. The surface decoration is known as taratara a Kae, 'the notching of Kae'. Kae had no canoe so he borrowed a pet whale. Instead of giving it back to its owner after his trip, he killed and ate it. The whale's owner sent his women to find Kae. The women were not sure what he looked like, but knew he had twisted teeth. Everywhere they went, the women did lewd dances to make people laugh and show their teeth. Kae fell into their trap, laughing, and they killed him.

The five brothers went fishing. Maui had to smuggle himself on board the canoe because the others were so tired of his tricks, they would not take him with them. When they found him hiding under a mat they had little option but to let him stay, but they would not give him a fish-hook. So Maui used the magic jaw-bone instead and, by dint of magic incantations, hooked and hauled up the huge fish named Te Ika a Maui (The Fish of Maui), which became the North Island of New Zealand. The canoe was raised high in the air on the peak of Mount Hikurangi. Before Maui could fetch a priest to sanctify the fish and divide it properly, the greedy brothers started cutting it up. The fish writhed and its skin wrinkled, and that is why the North Island of New Zealand is not flat but is thrown into hilly folds.

In another adventure, Maui, who was annoyed at the shortness of the day, persuaded his brothers to lie with him in wait for the sun, so they could snare the sun with the magic jaw-bone. They succeeded in snaring the sun, and they beat him so soundly that thenceforth he could only crawl across the heavens, so lengthening the hours of useful daylight.

One day Maui mischievously put out all the fires in the village. To save himself from well-merited retribution he set out to obtain a fresh supply of fire from his ancestress, Mahuika, the goddess of fire. She agreed to help him, but his continuing tricks so infuriated her, that she finally set all the forests on fire. Maui fled before the flames in the form of a hawk. He called on his ancestor Tawhiri-matea, the god of storms, to save him. The god deluged the land with rain. Now it was the fire's turn to flee.

Opposite left: Tekoteko, or roof finial from a Taupo storehouse. The storehouse was the esteemed, or tapu, building of the early nineteenth century. It belonged to the chief, who stored delicacies in it to be served to tribal guests. The figure is an ancestor of the Tuwharetoa tribe.

Opposite right: These eighteenth-century symbols of gods were placed outside a house of learning, to indicate what was being taught that day. The twisted stick represents Tawhirimatea, god of stormwinds; the straight stick is Tumatawenga, god of man and war; the stick with one swelling is Tane, god of the forests, and the wavy stick is Tangaroa, god of the sea. This is the only extant set known.

Right: The taumata atua of the god of agriculture, Rongo. Originally from Waitara in North Taranaki. The sculpture was a visible symbol to the god that his aid had been invoked to ensure a good crop of kumara. Its form is more that of a mauri, or soul, than of a crop figure.

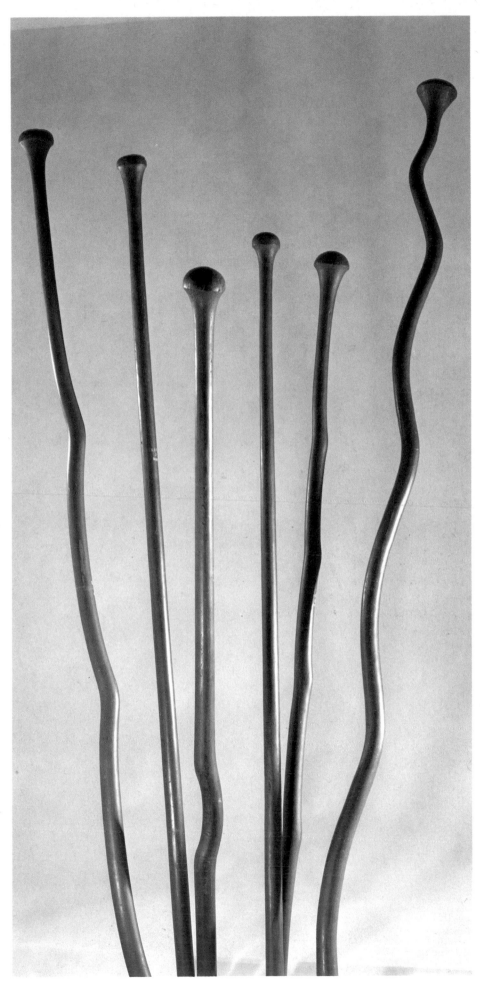

Tree after tree refused to give it protection; only the mahoe, totara, patete, pukatea and kaikomako agreed to grant shelter to the fire. Maui returned to the village empty-handed, but from that day forward, fire was obtained by rubbing a stick cut from one of the five 'fire trees' along a groove in another piece of wood.

Maui proposed to descend into the realm of Hine-nui-te-po, the Great Lady of the Darkness, the daughter and wife of Tane, and the goddess of death. Maui's mother had explained that, should he enter the goddess's womb and traverse her body to emerge through her mouth, the goddess would be vanquished. Armed with the enchanted jaw-bone and accompanied by a host of birds, the hero descended into the Underworld, where he found the dread goddess asleep.

'When you see me crawl into the vagina of the old chieftainess, whatever you do, do not laugh,' Maui warned his friends. 'If you laugh too soon, she will wake and kill me. But if you can keep quiet until I have emerged, I shall live and Hine-nui will die and man will live for ever.' Maui changed himself into a caterpillar and set about his task, but he looked so comical that little *tiwaiwaka*, the fantail, could not control his mirth. He laughed out loud. The goddess woke and crushed the interloper to death between her thighs. And that was the end of the demi-god Maui.

Gods need human interpreters according to Maori logic, for without such mediums they could not exist. 'Gods can and do die when there are no

Eighteenth-century feeding funnel. Funnels like this were usually used to feed liquid food to a chief while he was in the process of having his face tattooed. If food were to touch any part of the skin, it would diminish the mana of the chief, and during the time of tattooing especially, that could have catastrophic consequences. Feeding funnels were also used by other people when their faces were being tattooed, and when a priest or chief communicated with a god, he would be fed by another person through a funnel.

priestly mediums to keep them alive', insisted a witness at a nineteenth-century land court. The *tohunga,* or priests, were not a distinct social class though they were probably all of the *rangatira* or sub-chief class. First-born high chiefs also had a religious role. They inherited spiritual power, or *mana,* from the gods by reason of their primogeniture and usually received training in the schools of sacred learning together with the *tohunga.* After such training, they were empowered to perform certain ceremonies.

The term *tohunga,* when used without qualification, always denoted a priest. But the literal meaning of the word is 'expert', and skilled craftsmen were also termed *tohunga,* though always with a qualifying adjective. A *tohunga tarai waka,* for instance, was a master shipwright, a *tohunga whakairo* a skilled wood-carver and a *tohunga te moko* an expert tattooist.

The priest was regarded as the human receptacle of a god, the *waka atua,* literally the god's canoe. On important occasions he became possessed by the holy spirit and spoke with tongues. There were a number of grades of priesthood. The highest class went through long years of esoteric training; the lowest only read the stars and cast spells. Sorcery, or black magic, was not taught in the higher schools (though the greatest priests could practice it effectively upon occasion), but was taught in inferior establishments called *whare maire.* To work an inimical spell, a relationship had to be established with a malignant spirit, and some article of the subject's clothing or a portion of his hair or nails had to be obtained. No doubt, if the victim knew he was being bewitched the effect was intensified.

When officiating at major ceremonies the *tohunga* stripped off his clothing and either remained naked or donned a loincloth of fresh leaves, lest the everyday garments should defile his sacredness or *tapu* and so drain away his *mana,* his spiritual power.

The main method of influencing the gods was by intoning a *karakia,* or sacred chant. These were almost endless in their variety. *Karakia hono* united broken bones, *karakia ki rakau* gave power to wooden weapons, *karakia atahu* were love charms, and so on. Among what might be termed medical *karakia* here is one to relieve stomach ache:

What was the food
That entered your stomach
Causing trouble, causing disturbance,
Causing groans?
Perhaps it was . . .?

(Here follows a list of likely offending food items.) The chant concludes:

Oh, Oh, Oh,
You will recover
Oh you will recover.

In more martial vein, an incantation dedicating a boy-child to the war god, Tu, runs in part:

Proceed thou . . .
To become angry . . .
To become bold . . .
To kill men . . .
To enter forts . . .
To slay sentries . . .

(from Buck, *The Coming of the Maori*)

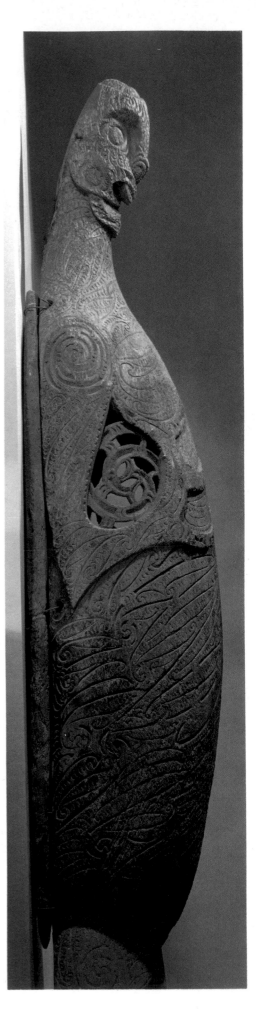

While *karakia* were invocations or prayers, they were not addressed directly to the god, for this would have been impertinent, a breach of good manners. Traditional Maori oratory was as much in evidence in *karakia* as it was in purely secular orations. References to genealogies, real or mythical, and to the great personages and incidents of myth and legend added weight and authority to the chants. *Karakia* constituted only one of the bridges that linked the interlocking worlds of gods and men, of *te kauae runga*, things spiritual, with *te kauae raro*, the concerns of the temporal world. The Maori saw these two worlds as aspects of one whole.

Few *karakia* were complete in themselves; ritual and ceremonial acts were integral parts of the invocation. The priest might stand with arms extended or with one arm pointing to the sky. In some war rituals the warriors knelt on one knee before him while he chanted the prayer. Earth from a sacred shrine, water for purification, fire to enhance the life principle or to destroy harmful influences, each had its symbolic role. Human hair was a potent substance, particularly that of an *ariki* (high chief), and above all the hair from his head, the head being the most *tapu* (sacred) part of the body. The hair of a *mata ika* ('first fish'), the first opponent slain in a battle, was the subject of special ceremony. It was customary also to burn a hair from one's head in a ritual fire when undertaking a perilous journey. The *taniwha* (monsters) that roused the sea to fury could be placated by plucking out a hair from one's head and casting it into the waters.

Nothing brings out better the non-material essence of Maori religion than the complete absence of imposing places of worship. Neither, as we have seen, did this highly artistic people have any penchant for carving graven images of their gods. Things spiritual, *te kauae runga*, were so much part of day-to-day life and of such inherent dignity, they did not need to be glorified through art. It was the sacredness of Maori *tuahu*, or shrines, that imposed awe and veneration, not their physical characteristics; they were, for the most part, but unworked standing stones or wooden posts.

In this, New Zealand was unique in Polynesia. Generally, the *marae*, or temple platform, was a majestic structure. In some island groups the *marae* itself was sacred. In others there was a separate altar called an *ahu* which stood on the *marae*. The New Zealand *marae* on the other hand, was simply a ceremonial ground situated before the clan or tribe's ceremonial house. It was the centre of political debate and oratory, but it was open to everyone and was wholly secular. The *tuahu* (shrine) was removed to a hidden sacred place, which was so highly charged with spiritual power as to be mortally perilous to the uninitiated.

Offerings to the gods were placed on the *tuahu* altar, but they might also be deposited in other appropriate places. Food items were the customary gifts; birds for Tane, fish for Tangaroa, kumara for Rongo, fern root for Haumia – and slain human beings, the food for Tu. Contestants in battle would complete for the first kill, so as to obtain the *mata ika*, the 'first fish', which was an offering that found much favour in the sight of Tu. In this case, there was no time to wait for a suitable altar; the priest tore out the slain warrior's heart and offered it up on the spot; later a lock of hair or a piece of flesh was brought home to the tribal altar. Before a major campaign, a slave or a captive was sacrificed to Tu. The gift of a dog sufficed for smaller raiding parties.

Human sacrifice, however, was far less prevalent in New Zealand than in other parts of Polynesia. Very occasionally a victim might be buried under the rear pole of a particularly important ceremonial house, but usually a stone *mauri* was adequate. The launching of a war canoe over a human victim was a more common practice. Generally, offerings to the gods were of a less lethal character – food, woven flax, even stones or leaves might be offered to any special trees or rock formations that symbolized the spirit of a particular territory. For *tuahu* altars were not the only sacred places. Many natural features of the land embodied their own essence of spiritual power, even if in lesser degree.

Apart from mediating with the gods, priests had the important task of

Left: Bone box from Waimamaku, Hokianga. In the Northland, bodies of chiefs were exposed on a platform until the flesh had gone. After cleaning, they were painted with red ochre and placed in a bone box in a cave. Below: Detail.

dealing with the spirits of the dead, with ghosts. People went in great fear of the spirits of the departed, especially of the newly deceased, who had not yet had time to descend into the realm of Night. Elaborate incantations and rituals by priests and lay individuals served a protective function. Yet ghosts were not necessarily malignant, though they were always possessed of awesome power which it was dangerous to encounter. Buck writes of his uncle who feared to go home at night because of a recent death. A cooked potato was given him by Buck's mother, who explained, 'The spirits will not come near cooked food. If you see one, rub the potato on your face.' The remedy, remarks Buck, was simple but effective.

No systems of rewards and punishments awaited the *wairua* or soul of a departed Maori. This *wairua* was a true soul, in that it survived death. But it could also leave the body temporarily during sleep. In dreams, the soul would wander abroad, sometimes bringing back valuable information, like the imminence of a hostile attack. After death the *wairua* tended to become malignant – hence the healthy respect for ghosts. Especially did this apply to the *wairua* of unborn children. On another plane, the spirits of important ancestors became deified and might be worshipped. Thus Ueneuku of Hawaiki, who may once have been a real chief, attracted his own human victims as a minor, but potent, god of war.

Devotion to distinguished human ancestors, especially to the founding fathers of *hapu,* (clans) or *iwi,* (tribes), took on a quality of piety and reverence not always accorded to the high gods themselves. Invocations to the latter were essentially designed to gain their favour by magic and ritual; prayers were not appeals for help in the Christian manner. But veneration for the mighty ancestors of old was bound up with their role as repositories of the *mana* or spiritual status of the tribe or clan. Their actual and legendary doings were frequently recalled in speech and song and were held up as sacred exemplars for the living. Their carved likenesses stood in ceremonial houses and tribal storehouses and often crowned the gateways of stockades. Upon these images the most renowned wood-carvers lavished their greatest skill.

Perhaps the most important concept governing Maori attitudes and actions was that of *tapu*, or sacredness. Both human beings and things could be *tapu* and the condition of *tapu* might be permanent or temporary. The rules of *tapu* were only flouted at risk of mortal danger.

All males except slaves were *tapu* to a greater or lesser extent, depending on their birth and status. The most sacred parts of the body were the head, back and sexual organs; the hands were moderately *tapu*, the feet not all. Women, apart from high-chieftainesses, did not possess the quality except at menstruation and childbirth. They were *noa*, the opposite of *tapu*.

Tapu flowed onto the objects that a person touched, or even onto those upon which his shadow chanced to fall. The sacredness of a high chief or priest was so formidable that during periods when he communicated with the gods, he had to be fed by another person with the aid of a stick or a funnel. Cooked food being particularly *noa*, the chief's sacred essence would drain away if he so much as touched anything so profane. A *tapu* person drinking from a gourd would hold it aloft so his lips should not touch the *noa* receptacle. Canoe-builders were purified in special ceremonies to render them *tapu*. Similarly, war parties were ritually cleansed before setting out, to place them under the *tapu* of Tu. On return from battle the blood *tapu* was removed, so that they could again consort with their families. The construction of a ceremonial house was always a solemn undertaking, the builders and wood-carvers being consecrated *tapu* for the task. While the work was in progress they must have no congress with women, nor must any woman set foot in the building. On completion of the building the *tapu* was removed by appropriate ritual. Then a chieftainess stepped over the threshold to show that the ceremonial house had been made *noa* and was now open to all.

As a broad generality, the sky and all things male tended towards *tapu*, while women and earthly objects of everyday use were mostly *noa*. Should a warrior be captured and enslaved, the high level of *tapu* that had been with him in battle drained utterly away. He became one with the women and, henceforth, engaged with them in such particularly *noa* undertakings as cooking.

Vega and Canopus were *tapu* stars, whose appearance in the night sky of an evening signalled the seasons for planting flax and for harvesting kumara, respectively. Birds, fish and eels were strictly *tapu* outside the recognized hunting or trapping seasons. Thus was a wise conservation measure maintained by fear of divine sanction. It is rather less obvious why particular rocks, trees, pools or hills were held to be *tapu*.

Death, too, was associated with formidable *tapu*. While lesser degrees of *tapu* could be lifted by the proper ceremony, a building where death had occurred was no longer safe to inhabit and had to be burned down. This was why, if a person became seriously ill in a ceremonial house, he was moved to a temporary shelter, so ensuring the preservation of the centre of community life.

The concept of *mana* is more difficult to define. It was a spiritual potency of divine origin conferred upon a human being. It was something very much more than merely status, power, prestige or self-confidence. High chiefs possessed it in large measure, and this was of great moment to their tribes, because the *mana* of chiefs flowed down to their followers. In this sense the tribe itself could be said to have *mana*.

Mana was not inviolable; it could be dissipated by the incorrect performance of ceremonies or by mistakes in *karakia* (sacred chants) or, even more disastrous, by the violation of some *tapu*. Then the power bestowed by the gods drained away, leaving the hapless mortal bereft of his spiritual potency. Not only human beings had *mana*. A *karakia* often had great *mana*, dependent on the 'innate virtue' of its words, though its efficacy seems to have been enhanced by the *mana* of the priest who composed or recited the chant.

Gods themselves had *mana*. When the Reverend Chapman attempted to convert the last pagan priest of the Arawa Tribe, the old *tohunga* demonstrated the power of his god by turning a dry leaf green. This was an impressive manifestation of the god's *mana*. When the missionary's deity failed to match the pagan *atua's* achievement, the old priest remained unconvinced by him, and continued to live in the faith of his fathers.

There were special rituals associated with birth and death, as there are throughout the world. When a child was twelve days old it was baptised in a sacred part of a stream in a ritual called *tohi*. The ritual removed the birth *tapu* and made the baby fit for the reception of divine influences. (While this may seem logically inconsistent to Westerners, the Maori were able to accept mutually contradictory concepts, without worrying about their incompatibility.) The *tohunga* dipped his hand in the stream, in which he was standing, and drew his wet hand across the face of the baby where it rested in the crook of his left arm, at the same time intoning an incantation. Apart from this important ceremony, a baby's sneeze had special significance. '*Tike mauri ora*,' its parents would exclaim – 'Sneeze, living soul.' For was not a sneeze the first sign of life that came from

Opposite: This is the actual hull of the war canoe of a dead chief. It has been cut in half and carved with figures representing the Underworld, and then erected as a memorial to the chief.

Below: A very early bone box, possibly dating to the sixteenth century, which was made to contain the bones of a child of chiefly rank. In style it is transitional between archaic and classical Maori art.

Hine-ahuone, the Earth-formed Maid, when Tane gave her breath?

Death came to the mighty
When Maui was strangled
by the Great Lady of the Night
And so remained in the world.

(from Buck, *The Coming of the Maori*)

The green leaves of the *kawakawa* symbolized death. Wailing and tears greeted the mourners who came to pay respects to the departed, for a copious flow of tears was said to 'avenge death'. Gifts were exchanged with the bereaved. The *tangi*, or mourning ceremony, was (and still is) one of the great occasions for Maori oratory, and it is not surprising that some of the most moving Maori poems were laments.

Alas, the bitter pain
which gnaws within,
For the canoe which is wrecked,
For the friend who has gone.

(from Buck, *The Coming of the Maori*)

While the *tangi* took place everywhere in New Zealand, burial customs varied from place to place. In some districts inhumation was the rule, in others the corpse was hidden in a cave until only the bare bones remained. These were then returned to the *marae*, cleaned, oiled and painted with red ochre. After a sorrowful ceremony the relics were consigned to their last secret resting place, often encased in a superbly carved 'bone box' and accompanied by weapons and greenstone heirlooms.

Meanwhile the soul of the departed, sped by the orator's admonition, '*Haere ki te Po!*' ('Go to the Underworld!'), was making its lonely way towards Te Rerenga-wairua where the northern mainland ends. As it neared the point of departure the spirit deposited a branch or frond it had brought from home as a last reminder. It crossed the stream called Water of the Underworld, traversed the Twilight Sands and passed over another brook, the Waters of Lamentation, to reach the final promontory that jutted out over the Great Ocean of Kiwa.

Sir Peter Buck once made a reconnaissance this far (he has since completed the journey). He gazed at the ancient *pohutukawa* tree, along whose roots the spirit at death would climb down into the sea-swirled kelp. Then, lifting his eyes, he spied the Three Kings Islands, with the island of Ohau standing out clearly. The spirit would ascend the highest hill on that island for one last look back at the land it would never see again. Hence the lines of the lament:

Ohau in the distance –
Last hill of farewell!

(from Buck, *The Coming of the Maori*)

From Ohau, the spirit's way lay across the western ocean along the track of the westering sun, to join, in the far-off spirit land, its kinsmen of ancestral Hawaiki.

Parua Bay, on the north-east coast of the North Island.

TE KAUAE RARO
Earthly Things

There is a temptation to speak of Classic Maori culture as if it were something uniform and static. This was not so. While the transition from the Archaic to the Classic can be identified as revolutionary in terms of population expansion and north-to-south migration, and in terms of tools, agriculture, canoes, fort-building and warfare, the changes were by no means complete in most of the South Island or in the Chathams where a different culture developed. Neither did the process of change cease after the sixteenth century. The Maori with their double canoes encountered by Tasman in 1642, for instance, seem to have been far removed in organization from the people Cook saw 150 years later. Not only was Classic Maori culture as a whole continually developing and changing in all its aspects, but there were marked regional and tribal differences, even within the Iwitini climatic region.

The extended family, *whanau*, was the basis of Maori society. Parents, children, grandparents, uncles, aunts and cousins all dwelt in a close-set cluster of little houses. Cousins and siblings were equally 'brothers' and 'sisters', and uncles and aunts were considered 'mothers' and 'fathers'.

The family met as a group to decide important matters, though the last word rested with the *kaumatua*, the male head of the family. He also acted as its spokesman in the wider forum of the clan meeting.

The place of an individual in the system depended upon two factors: first, his seniority, both his personal seniority and that of his descent line (the most distinguished being *rangatira* or chiefly lines); and secondly, upon the generation to which he belonged.

An elder brother or sister (or cousin) was termed *tuakana*, and a younger *teina*. This senior and junior relationship applied to their children and children's children as well. Down through the generations the descendents of the *tuakana* remained forever socially superior to the descendants of the *teina*, and this held good regardless of the individuals' ages.

This seems straightforward, but a younger son (*teina*) could easily be so much younger than an elder (*tuakana*) that his children would be the same age as the *tuakana's* grandchildren. The son of the *teina* would then be 'father' to the grandson of the *tuakana* because the latter belonged to the next generation. Yet the *teina* line itself would still be junior. Who then, son of the junior line or grandson of the senior, should enjoy superior status? It can readily be seen that anomolies and room for dispute abounded. To add to the possibilities of confusion, descent could be traced in the female line as well as the male. Children could also be adopted into a family. It is no wonder that lengthy and complex genealogies were

At Donnelly's Crossing, in the north-west of the North Island, two kauri trees, each with twin trunks, have grafted themselves together. They are called the Four Sisters. Kauri trees play an important part in Maori history, practically, in terms of economy, but also in terms of their mythological significance. Many kauri trees are 1500 years old and more, and the Maori have given names to all the old trees. The Four Sisters seem symbolic of Maori history, being roughly the same age, of separate trunks, and yet growing together.

Above: Bird-shaped okewa club from Waitangi in the Chatham Islands. The Moriori people of the Chathams retained a variety of the archaic Maori culture long after that culture had disappeared from the North Island.

Opposite: Te Hau ki Turanga meeting house. The ancestors on the wall slabs are connected to the main ridge pole by painted rafters. The painted design on the ridge pole and rafters is derived from the tendrils of a gourd plant and represents the genealogical tree.

Below: An early canoe prow from Doubtless Bay in the far north. The sculpture is transitional between Archaic and later Maori art.

recited, going back twenty or more generations, but even these could not always resolve conflicts.

The *hapu* or clan was the most important Maori social unit in terms of economic undertakings, ceremonial and religious gatherings and war. It was extremely close-knit and was made up of a number of extended families to a total of perhaps five hundred people. Every member of a *hapu* (or his spouse) traced his or her descent from a common ancestor, through either the male or the female line. The *ariki,* or chief, came from the senior *rangatira* (aristocratic) line. Marriage was generally within the clan, but not always. In 'outside' unions it was usual, but by no means invariable, for the woman to move to her husband's *hapu*. Those who did marry into another clan retained their former affiliation, including rights to the use of land. Within a generation or two, however, these rights were considered to have lapsed.

The *iwi*, or tribe, was a much looser structure than the clans of which it was composed. Membership was again based on descent from a common ancestor but, in this case, a considerably more remote and sometimes semi-mythical one, generally from one of the traditional founding canoes like *Arawa* or *Aotea*. The extent to which members of a tribe acted together in peace and war depended to a very large extent on the *mana* and personal quality of the high-born *ariki* who stood at its head. Tribes, and sometimes confederations of tribes, would unite against a common enemy. But bloody strife between *hapu* of the same tribe was all too frequent.

The Maori kinship system was thus an all-embracing one, relating every individual in some degree with every other one, at varying degrees of remove from family, clan and tribe, and linking every individual to a line of ancestors stretching back to the mists of Hawaiki. At the same time, ambiguous titles to seniority, debatable rights of people who married or were adopted into *hapu*, and the manipulation of the system by individuals of ambition were potent causes of almost perennial strife.

Maori society was stratified into an aristocratic *rangatira* class and a lower *tutua* class. *Rangatira* were of the *tuakana* (senior descent) line. They consciously maintained and strengthened their status by means of arranged marriages and by constantly striving after excellence in such socially prestigious fields as tribal politics, oratory and war. But despite distinctions of rank and birth, there was no difference in the tasks performed by members of the two classes in the fields, fishing grounds and forests. Chiefs and commoners alike cleared the scrub and dug the heavy ground on their garden plots. There were no special terms of respect used in addressing social superiors, for all, in varying degree, shared in the *tapu* and *mana* of Tane. Aristocratic women, too, performed the same work as their humbler sisters. There was a sharp division, however, between tasks proper to men and those performed by women.

An individual's personal achievements brought him increased *mana*, and so enhanced the status of his relatives and augmented their *mana*. Family honour – *mana* – was very precious to the Maori. Strict tally was kept of infringements of family and tribal honour. Vengeance varied from token gestures to full-scale war and defeats or humiliations might only be avenged after several generations. Less serious slights and insults could be neutralized by *muru*, or formal plundering raids, whereby *utu* (recompense, revenge) would be obtained. More heinous offences called for a *taua*, or war party, and *utu* could then only be achieved by the shedding of blood.

Buck's account of a latter-day *muru* throws light on Maori attitudes

concerning both revenge and the significance of marriage in society.

The occasion was that of a wife leaving her husband for a lover in another tribe. This concerned the community because Maori marriage was a formal agreement not between two individuals but between two family groups. Thus an affair of a husband or wife which involved another *hapu* or tribe, was the concern of the whole aggrieved extended family or sub-tribe, and the *hapu* would dispatch a raiding party to the offender's village to exact recompense. The people of that *hapu* were held collectively responsible, as the culprit was a part of their group. The right of the raiding party was usually recognized, and no resistance was offered.

Buck's party armed themselves symbolically and marched onto the offenders' *marae*, where they executed a fierce war dance before the assembled villagers. The erring wife and her lover had long since fled to distant parts, but this was immaterial.

> [The raiders' chiefs] made fiery speeches accusing the local tribe of guilt in sexual matters, punctuating their remarks with libidinous songs . . . The village chiefs admitted their fault and then proceeded to lay various articles before us in payment, such as jade ornaments, bolts of print cloth and money in pound notes. Each individual, as he or she advanced to the pile, called out the nature of their contribution. Some gave horses and cattle . . . We then rubbed noses with our hosts, engaged in amicable conversation, partook of a feast provided for us, and returned [home].

Buck draws special attention to a highly significant line in a speech made by one of his own party's chiefs: 'The clouds of heaven settle only on the peaks of lofty mountains and the clouds of trouble settle only on the heads of high chiefs.' This signified that if the family of the offender were of poor status, the war party would not have deigned to visit it. The tribe accepted the clouds of trouble cheerfully, as tributes to its prestige. Indeed, its *mana* had been enhanced by the very magnificence of the gifts it had offered in recompense.

The active leadership of the tribe was generally a male prerogative, but it sometimes happened that the firstborn of the senior *rangatira* line was a female. She was then accorded the greatest respect as *wahine-ariki* (woman chief). The degree to which such a one wielded power varied markedly from tribe to tribe. The east coast tribes revered such high-born women and allowed them to speak in council on the *marae*. On rare occasions a female *ariki* became in fact – as well as in name – the chief of the people.

Slaves were in no sense a separate hereditary caste in Maori society. They were outside the pale and excluded from the kinship system themselves. Slaves were usually men and women captured in war and spared to perform menial tasks. In fact, their capture was sometimes deliberately undertaken to augment the labour force. With enslavement a man lost all his *tapu* and *mana* and was assigned to women's work, cooking, carrying water and firewood, and to heavy labour in the fields. Slaves had no rights and might on occasion be sacrificed or otherwise killed. As a rule, however, they were well fed, and treated kindly enough. It is noteworthy that their demeanour differed not at all from that of free men. They walked erect and addressed their owners without a hint of subservience. (This

Te Anau Fiordland. 'The clouds of heaven settle only on the peaks of lofty mountains and the clouds of trouble settle only on the heads of high chiefs.'

behaviour was commented upon most unfavourably by Charles Darwin, who considered such familiarity of manner unbecoming in the lower orders.) Rather surprisingly, slaves were perfectly free to marry into the *hapu* of their captors and the children of such unions were accorded full status as free men and women, even if the 'bar sinister' of slave ancestry precluded them from rising to the highest rank.

Maori marriage was a contract between families and wider groups, which had widely ramifying implications as to property rights and the interlinking of descent groups. Oddly enough, though it was such a socially significant institution, there was no actual ceremony; an exchange of gifts made the union legal, but it was the acceptance by the community of a couple sleeping together that counted. Generally, except

Paua shell cloakpin from Northland. Paua is a local species of abalone. This pin has a cord-hole at the top where it was tied to the cloak that pinned it together.

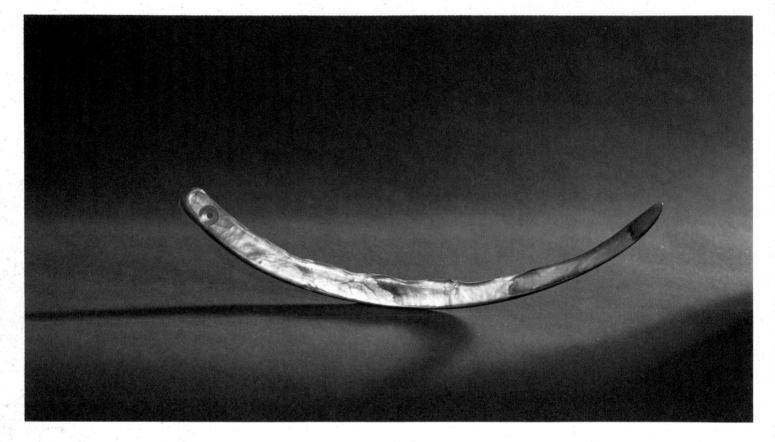

Opposite: Panel from the Te Hau ki Turanga meeting house, showing an ancestress breastfeeding her child.

when high-born girls were married to cement tribal alliances, the personal preference of the couple was a major factor. Marriages within the *hapu* won approval because they avoided split loyalties and property complications. Second cousins were the closest relatives permitted to marry each other.

Almost complete sexual freedom was permitted to both sexes before marriage, except that high-born girls were required to be discreet. Exceptional was the *puhi* (tribal virgin), whose chastity was jealously guarded until her hand should be bestowed in a marriage of high policy for the benefit of the whole people. Chastity was a quality not normally much esteemed, but, in the case of a *puhi*, it was part of the tribal *mana,* and retribution was apt to be severe if a *puhi* fell from grace. It is a relief to be able to record that several such were quick-witted enough to blame their pregnancy on divine visitations and to have their stories accepted!

Sexual freedom ceased abruptly with marriage. Monogamy was the norm for commoners, polygamy for chiefs, who generally had two wives, but sometimes as many as ten. The pleasures of variety apart, polygamy placed more labour at the chief's disposal to help meet his many obliga-

tions in dispensing hospitality, contributing a chiefly share to feasts and dispensing such ceremonial gifts as mats and cloaks. Polygamy was at the root of most domestic strife. The senior wife might bully her junior, or the older wife might be supplanted in the husband's affections. Matahira of the Ngaati Porou was senior wife to the chief Te Kotiri. Her lamentation when he stopped sleeping with her in favour of a younger woman ends with the poignant line, 'Alas, the wretchedness of a husband shared!'

The division of labour between men and women was sharply defined. Men felled trees, burnt off fern and scrub, and loosened the soil for planting; women then planted and subsequently cared for the kumara crop. Fern rhizomes were dug by men, collected and carried home by women. Men usually snared birds but women sometimes participated, being allotted the smaller trees. Open-sea fishing was men's work. Women were equally adept at handling canoes, however, and thought nothing of bringing cooked food out to warriors at sea, since the warriors could carry nothing cooked on the sacred war canoes. Men dove for rock lobster and deep-water *paua* (abalone), while women caught fresh-water crayfish and gathered shellfish in the inter-tidal zone. Either sex might collect berries, and women could help haul logs from the forest for house-building, but not for making canoes. The distinction between men's and women's work being based as much on *tapu* as on physical strength, women could have nothing to do with the building of meeting-houses or canoes. There were no female carvers, tattooists or warriors. Weaving and cloak-making, on the other hand, were mainly feminine occupations.

Cooking was the sole prerogative of women and slaves. Crushed fern root (*aruhe*) was roasted over charcoals, and other cooking was done in an earth oven (*hangi* or *umu*). Wood was piled high in a circular pit about a metre in diameter and smooth non-friable stones were placed on top. After the wood had been burnt and the stones were thoroughly heated, food was placed on them between layers of leaves. Water was sprinkled on freely, and the whole was covered with plaited flax mats and earth to seal in the steam. The cooking time was generally about two hours.

Fire was produced by friction with the fire-plough method. A hardwood stick was rubbed along a groove in a softwood board until the wood-dust smouldered and was carefully blown into flame on a pile of tinder – an operation more readily described than carried out!

Food was normally served on plaited flax platters which were disposable, so as to accommodate the demands of *tapu*.

High-born women have to be considered separately because, while subjected to exactly the same restrictions as other women, they had certain secular and ritual functions that were important to the whole community.

On the secular plane, the daughters of chiefs were often given to the more powerful *ariki*, as secondary wives to cement alliances, or, temporarily, as extremely gracious tokens of hospitality. After military defeat or deadlock, such daughters would be handed over to the erstwhile enemy in the hope of cementing peace. The practice was regarded as a highly effective one. As Te Heuheu said to his Ngati Kahungunu opponents after peace had been sealed in this manner, 'Now we will make peace for ever, for our daughter made peace, and a woman's peace is a lasting peace.'

The ritual role of *rangatira* women involved the lifting of *tapu* from completed meeting-houses, canoes and forts and the mitigation, in certain circumstances, of *tapu* associated with food, sickness and death. Although women very rarely took any physical part in warfare, they participated in the war *haka* (dances) and often incited the warriors from the sidelines, as it were. Women who were consanguineous to both parties

in a war were allowed to pass freely across the battle lines and, not infrequently, they acted as secret peace envoys.

At puberty, women, especially of the higher class, had their lips tattooed. When a high chief's eldest daughter reached puberty, the occasion demanded that a human victim, specially brought in by a raiding party, should be slain and eaten. The same rite accompanied the piercing of her ears.

A high-born woman was entitled to such privileges as being carried in a litter on formal occasions and wearing the most precious tribal ornaments when acting as a ceremonial hostess to visiting tribes. The head of a defeated chief, elaborately decorated with feathers, was ceremoniously placed before the leading woman of the tribe as a mark of respect; or if the hostilities had been to avenge wrongs done to her, she might claim the prerogative of herself killing the captured chief. One last dubious privilege of a chieftainess, one not necessarily honoured, was the senior wife's obligation to commit suicide upon the death of her husband.

Kumara and *aruhe* (fern root) cultivation was the rock on which Classic Maori economy rested. Kumara-planting time in spring was heralded by a mackerel sky, which had the appearance of a heavenly kumara plot, and was naturally interpreted as an invitation by the gods to begin planting.

But planting would have been unproductive in most parts of New Zealand had it not been for the soil-enrichment and tuber-storage techniques that had been so patiently and ingeniously developed. Fifty types of soil were recognized and very large areas of land were modified. This was most commonly accomplished by spreading sand and gravel, enriched with charcoal, to a depth of 3 to 4 centimetres (1.2 to 1.6 inches) over the stiff clay, underlying the soil. Some 200 hectares (5000 acres) of the mid-Waikato plain alone were treated in this way – a stupendous feat of labour.

The final step before planting was to break up the soil. A stepped digging stick (*ko*) was driven three times into the ground and the soil levered up and loosened. The soil was then pulverized with a wooden club, after which it was further worked and loosened and any roots removed. Finally, small mounds were built, ready to receive the seed tubers. Special *tapu* protected the workers, and god symbols were placed around the plots.

Kumara and fern root, under the protection of their respective gods, Rongo and Haumia, were the staple cultigens of New Zealand; the gourd, which had accompanied the early Maori from the tropics, was widely used for food storage and as a drinking vessel; a few taro and yams were grown.

But the New Zealand woodlands were bountiful. A whole host of berries were important items of diet. Some, like the *karaka*, required elaborate preparation; it had to be cooked in an *umu* for upwards of twenty-four hours to destroy the prussic acid in the kernels, before being stored in water for off-season consumption. Similarly, the poisonous seeds of the *tutu* had to be removed before the berries became edible. Other bush foods were the roots and pollen of the bulrush (*raupo*), the pith, roots and shoots of various ferns, cabbage-tree roots and shoots and the heart of *nikau* (palm).

Edible mammals were limited to the imported dogs and rats, which were readily taken in traps, and man himself.

Fowling and fishing made major contributions to the Maori diet, for

Tutoko River, Fiordland.

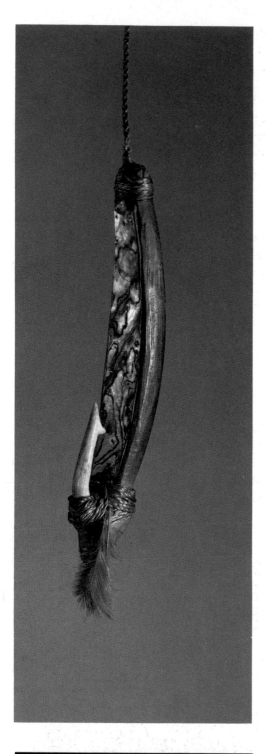

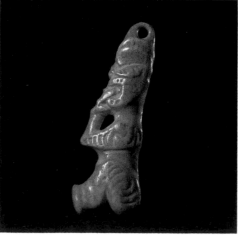

nowhere in New Zealand did the transition from hunting, fishing and gathering to agriculture become complete.

There was not much the Maori did not know about his land and its resources. He had names for a hundred birds and was equally knowledgeable as to the useful qualities of rock, bone, timber, and indeed, anything else in the environment. Birds of the bushlands, marshes and sea-cliffs were taken seasonally; at all other times they were protected by strict *tapu*. Favourite methods employed in the forest were snaring and spearing.

Perch snares of various kinds were used to catch bush-parrots and sometimes wood-pigeons. The perch was hooked to a branch or else attached to a long pole and placed in a tree-top the birds frequented. A cord with a running noose was looped to hang down on either side of the perch and the end led down to the waiting fowler, who crouched on a specially built platform. A decoy parrot, held by a leg-ring, was commonly used. The fowler irritated the parrot, so it would attract the wild birds with its squawking. As soon as an unwary one alighted on the snare, the noose was drawn tight around its leg, and its cries would bring more curious victims to nearby fatal perches. There was also a noose snare which acted automatically. These were just two among a whole gamut of ingenious devices. Apart from snares, a 9 metre (30 foot) bird spear with a barbed bone point was a favourite implement for impaling wood-pigeons in the upper branches.

Fish, both salt- and fresh-water species, were taken by a wide variety of techniques: line-fishing with baited hooks from convenient rocks or from canoes; trolling with bone-pointed lures from swift-moving canoes; seine and hand-nets; traps of different sorts and eel-weirs. Nets were made from green flax to save unnecessary labour, but lines had to be more durable and so were twisted into cords from dressed flax-fibre.

Effective methods for preserving food were invented and widely used in New Zealand. Fish and eels were hung out to sun-dry on racks, the precise procedure varying with the species. Sharks, for instance, were dried whole except for the heads, eels and scale fish were split open before drying and whitebait was first cooked. Abalone were also cooked and then threaded on strips of flax to dry. Birds and rats were cooked in gourds and preserved in their own fat in kelp bags. Kumara were stored underground. Special storehouses called *pataka,* some richly carved, were built to hold the preserved food, which was an important tribal asset.

Canoes loomed very large in Maori life. The tribes themselves traced descent from the distinguished ancestors of the founding canoes. Although long-distance, open-sea voyaging had been abandoned long before the Classic Maori period, canoes remained indispensable for fishing, transport and war.

Simple dugouts, *waka tiwai,* sufficed for general use on lakes and rivers. The larger fishing canoes, *waka tete,* which were sometimes up to 14 metres (46 feet) in length, were used for off-shore fishing and coastal transport. Freeboard was increased by the provision of gunwale strakes, the seams being sealed with outer and inner battens. A bow piece with a transverse washboard served to deflect head seas. There was a stern piece which was generally uncarved. As with all Maori craft, propulsion was mainly by paddle. Sails, when used at all, were of the extremely ancient Austronesian type, simple inverted triangles made of plaited flax.

The war canoe, or *waka taua,* was of the same general design as the *waka tete.* But it resembled it much as a hawk does a hen. War canoes were built from the magnificent kauri or totara trees and were often 24 metres (80 feet) long. They were the pride of the Maori and were among the most precious possessions of *hapu* and tribe. They were hedged around

Opposite above: Nineteenth-century lure for catching kahawai, Bay of Plenty. It is made from wood faced with a plate of Paua shell. The point is bone, the cord is flax, and it originally had a kiwi-feather lure at the back. Spinners of the same type, but now made in plastic, are still being used to catch kahawai.

with powerful *tapu* and were possessed of great *mana*. Upon the decoration the most accomplished wood-carvers lavished their greatest skill, and the carved bow and stern pieces are among the finest examples of Maori art. Buck wrote with feeling, 'Manned by a double row of tattooed warriors with their paddles flashing in perfect time to the canoe chants of a leader standing amidship with a quivering jade club, the speeding war canoe must have offered an inspiring yet awesome sight.'

Individual men and women had their own personal possessions; clothing, ornaments (though some might be family heirlooms), weapons and the like. Family property would comprise implements and utensils, pits and storehouses for their own produce, perhaps a simple dug-out (canoe) or two and a small eel-weir. Over and above these, resources were the property of the sub-tribe or *hapu* (clan) or of the *iwi* (tribe). It was these larger units that allocated the land the family cultivated and any forest or marine resources it was entitled to exploit.

As to land, the concept of 'ownership' did not exist. The land was part of the living essence of the tribe. It was the home of the gods. Tane's home was the forest, Rongo's was the kumara gardens and the potent spirits of ancestors dwelt in all the *tapu* places. The recognized symbol of occupancy was 'keeping the fires burning'. When, every few years, the kumara fields had to be allowed to lie fallow and cultivation shifted to new clearings, fires were periodically lit on the former sites of fields and villages so that the land rights 'should not grow cold'. Rights to land usage were vested in the *ariki* (including female *ariki*), but this was a sacred trust the *ariki* held on behalf of the *hapu*. Nonetheless, although technically a family or even a *hapu* did not own land but only owned the rights to the use of certain fields and gardens, these rights were jealously guarded and the source of endless manoeuvring, quarrels and war.

Trade, except in greenstone (local jade), was not highly developed in New Zealand, but ceremonial gift exchange served many of the same

Opposite below: A tiny human-bone tiki pendant, probably from the north-west tip of the South Island, as this type of small pendant in soapstone or bone is a peculiarity of the area. This one depicts an ancestor of the Ngati Apa or the Ngai Tumatokokiri tribe, both of which were conquered early in the nineteenth century by tribes from Taranaki. The tongue stuck out indicates surprise or aggression, and is used almost exclusively on ancestral images.

Right: Hei matau (fish-hook) pendant made of nephrite, given by a Ngapuhi chief to a British captain in 1834. Combining the fish-hook shape with the tiki, this is a unique ornament.

purposes and was an important part of Maori culture. Socially necessary exchanges took the place of 'commercial' trade. In the first place, there was a system equivalent to payment for services. *Tohunga* tattooists, adze-makers, shipwrights, builders, carvers and the like were rewarded for their work with gifts. There was never any bargaining, nor was any fee stipulated, but everyone knew what constituted a suitable present, and the more generous the offering, the more *mana* accrued to the giver. Favourite gifts were elaborately worked garments, jade ornaments and preserved food delicacies.

Gifts were exchanged among neighbours of the same *hapu*, the recipient's obligation being to present an object in return of equal, or greater, value. The return gift was usually given later to avoid any appearance of unseemly haste in discharging an obligation. Chiefly gifts were presented on behalf of one tribe to another, on such ceremonial occasions as *tangi* for important chiefs, or when tribal alliances were in the offing. It was this custom which was mainly responsible for the distribution of artifacts and products regionally and nationally. Members of one tribe, for instance, might have a reputation as skilled canoe builders, members of another as workers in greenstone. Regional access to resources also varied, so that muttonbirds, dried eels, greenstone and kumara were all objects of gift exchange.

The term *kainga*, living-place, denoted a dwelling or group of dwellings making up an unfortified village or settlement. This was the only type of community known to the Moa Hunters, and it is probable that most or all of their *kainga* were but seasonally occupied. The advent of warfare as an institution caused many *kainga* to be abandoned in favour of fortified villages, or *pa*. Unfortified *kainga* settlements still continued to exist near cultivations and fishing-grounds, but they would never be built very far away from the palisades of the protecting fortress, into which the inhabitants could retire at the first threat of attack. *Pa* were permanently occupied and, in some localities, wholly incorporated and replaced the *kainga*.

Dwelling-houses were very small rectangular structures built of split timber, poles or rush bundles. They were lined inside with the trunks of tree fern or with rushes. Cooking places and food storage structures were entirely separate for reasons of *tapu*. So were privies. The Maori were meticulous as to the disposal of excreta, which were never allowed to compromise the *mana* of the community.

The *whare whakairo*, or carved meeting-house which stood at the edge of the ceremonial ground, was richly carved and decorated, and was the repository of the carved images of famous ancestors. Venerated repository of tradition that it was, and is, the meeting-house that came into existence in the nineteenth century represented an indigenous, entirely Maori response to the large houses of the Europeans.

A *pa* might sometimes be built on flat ground defended by high stockades, watch towers and fighting platforms, but the majority were situated on hills, spurs, cliff-girt promontories or islands in swamps or lakes where natural features assisted defensive works. The defences comprised ditches, scarps, ramparts and wooden stockades, engineered with such sophistication that during the wars of the nineteenth century the pathetically ill-armed defenders of more than one *pa* were able to withstand for days the fire of British cannon.

Goose Bay, a bird sanctuary for birds to nest and rest after migrating. Generally speaking, the Maori were careful not to overkill.

TOHUNGA WHAKAIRO

Carvers of Tane

Carving in New Zealand was an exclusively male profession, for at all times it attracted *tapu*, and women were *noa*. Master craftsmen were termed *tohunga whakairo,* or specialists in carving. There was a religious connotation in this use of '*tohunga*'. Carvers were regarded as of *rangatira* rank and some were high *ariki ;* they were possessed of not a little *mana*. The entire tool-kit of the craftsman-artist, the work that was in progress and the carvers themselves were *tapu* to a degree dependent on the sacredness of the project. Ancestral figures crowning stockades or in meeting-houses, end-pieces of war canoes, decorated boxes destined to hold the bones of great chiefs, all these were *tapu* and any violation of them, even if unwitting, would bring calamity on the community.

The tall conifer, totara, and the kauri pine, which only grows north of Auckland, were the preferred woods for carving (as they were for canoe-building). Totara could be split readily, was soft enough to work with stone tools and was also durable. Special purposes demanded appropriate timber. Thus heavily knotted hardwoods made the best war-clubs.

The art of carving was by no means confined to working in wood. Stone, bone, whales' teeth, and seal ivory were made into ornaments, implements and weapons. Greenstone *hei-tiki* pendants (*hei*, to suspend; *tiki*, human figure) were highly esteemed as family and tribal heirlooms. The greenstone *mere* or stabbing club (called a *patu* when made in other materials) was harmonious in form and perfectly balanced – and deadly at close quarters.

Apprenticeship to a master was the means whereby a youth became a carver. He would be accepted much more readily for training if he were a close relative or at least in the same *hapu* as the master, and *rangatira* status was an asset. Where there was a strong carving tradition, especially where there was a functioning 'school' gathered around a well-known master, a gifted and pious young man could not fail to prosper. He would have to be gifted if he were to excel, because every male Maori was something of a craftsman. He would need to be pious, because the carving of sacred images demanded strict compliance with *tapu* if the gods were to bestow their *mana*. The existence of a school or team was important, because major works like meeting-houses were co-operative efforts under the direction of a master. The early nineteenth-century Gisbourne chief, Raharuhi Rukupo, had the help of no less than eighteen assistant carvers in executing the famous Te Hau ki Turanga (Spirit of Turanga) meeting-house which graces the National Museum in Wellington.

The story of the Hotunui meeting-house (now in Auckland Museum) illustrates the powerful influence exerted by *tapu* and *mana*, even as late

The main support post in front of the Te Hau ki Turanga meeting house, with a self-portrait of the chief carver, Raharuhi Rukupo at the far side of the door. This meeting house was built at Manutuke, near Gisborne, in 1842. It is the earliest meeting house of modern times.

Detail of the tattoo on the forehead of Rukupo. Raharuhi Rukupo was a chief of the Ngati Kaipoho tribe, and it was he who planned, directed and did much of the actual carving of Te Hau ki Turanga.

as 1878, when the house was built. Seventy Ngatiawa from a number of *hapu* were building the house under the direction of several master carvers. The work at first prospered but, after an inadvertent breach of *tapu*, it was found that the massive roof beam, which symbolized the spine of the ancestor for whom the house was named, could not be raised. This account is by Mokomoko, daughter of the head carver in charge, the high chief Apanui.

When an attempt was made to lift the ridge-pole it failed; then we sent Paroto Manutawhiorangi who uttered an incantation, or *karakia*, called *Tehuti o Tainui* (the raising of Tainui), and lo! the great tree was lifted up quickly and easily. Such was the power of magic as exercised by Maori priests of old. During the building a number of Ngatiawa workmen were smitten with sudden illness, which was attributed to their having burned in a cooking-fire some chips from

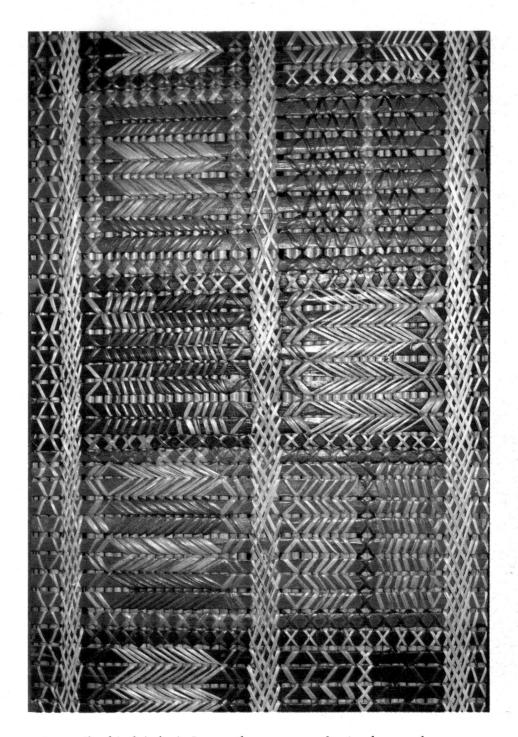

Tukutuku panels, or decorated reed panels such as this were always made by women for the walls of meeting houses. This one was made by the Ngati Maru women at Thames in 1878, for the meeting house Hotunui.

Apanui's chisel (*whao*). It was the women who inadvertently committed sacrilege, and the sickness which fell upon our people was termed a *mate-ruahine*. When several persons had died, my brother Wepiha came to me at dawn of day saying, '*Kua ngaro a Ngatiawa* (Ngatiawa will be annihilated). Hasten you quickly to remove the spell caused by the desecration of the work of our father's chisel.' I hurried to the spot, and in the midst of the assembly a small fire was made of chips from the carvings, and two kumara roasted therein, which were offered to me to eat. I trembled with fear, lest death should come to me also; but the old men said, 'Fear not, you are equal in mana to Apanui, your father, and you alone can remove this spell which is destroying Ngatiawa.' I then ate the roasted food and the epidemic ceased. Soon the house was completed and Wepiha summoned a *tohunga* called Mohi Taikoreka from Opotiki to perform the ceremonies called '*whare kara*' – i.e. making the house '*noa*',

removing the *tapu* etc. After this was done, and the men had entered and eaten food in the house, three women (myself, Kitemate Kirita-hanga, and Mere Taipari) were sent for to *takahi te paepae* (to tread on or cross over the threshold, and thus remove the enchantment which debars women from entering a sacred house until this ceremony is ended), for, as you know, the ridge-pole would sag down in the middle and destroy the appearance of the house were this ceremony disregarded. As the morning star (*Kopu*) rose, we, the three women, crossed over the threshold which Te Raihi, of Ngatihaua, had *tapa'd* (called) Hape Koroki, and then the *mana o te whakairo* (the sacredness of the carving) was subjugated, overcome, and women generally were free to enter and eat within the house.

(From T. T. Barrow, *Maori Wood Sculpture*)

The art of adzing was regarded as the primary skill of a Maori carver and the adze was his most important tool. Adzes ranged from those with blades weighing around 100 grams (4 oz) to massive two-handed types with stone heads of 5 kilograms (10 lb) or more. As mentioned earlier, the gouging adze of the Moa Hunter canoe-builder gradually gave way to the wood-cutting adze of the Classic period. A Classic Maori carving was begun by rough dressing the timber with a heavy adze, then smaller adzes took over the blocking-out stage. The chisel took the place of the gouging canoe-building adze of the Archaic period; the mallet and chisel were the fine tools *par excellence* of the wood-carver.

There was a great variety of chisels (*whao*) made of basalt or greenstone. Some greenstone chisels were perforated at the butt end and worn by craftsmen as ear ornaments when not otherwise in use. Whether this was a badge of office or a means of safe-guarding valuable tools, we do not know.

The cord drill was used to drill holes in stone, bone and shell. The drill had a wooden shaft or spindle, up to a metre long, a balance weight, a stone point and pulling cords. The flake stone point was lashed to the shaft with flax-fibre cord. The balance weight consisted of two stones, two pieces of heavy wood, or a circular hoop of supplejack attached to the spindle by eight spokes. A twisted cord was tied by its middle to the top end of the spindle, thus providing two pulling cords. To use the drill, the point was placed in a pre-formed depression in the object to be bored and rotated by hand to wind up the cords. Holding a knotted end in each hand, the cords were pulled outwards in opposite directions with just enough strength to unwind the cords by rotating the spindle and causing its momentum to rewind the cords. The cords were pulled again, which caused the spindle to rotate in the opposite direction and rewind the cords. The strength of the outward pull and the subsequent slackening of tension to let the cords rewind had to be judged to a nicety to keep the spindle rotating in alternate directions with each pull.

The cord drill is believed to have been the only type used in prehistoric New Zealand. The pump drill is thought to have been a European introduction.

Carved meeting-houses were and still remain repositories of tribal tradition, myth and history. Here came together in one place the finest wood-carvers, skilled painters of rafter designs and weavers of mats and decorated reed wall-panels, this last being a female contribution, once a

The Te Hau ki Turanga meeting house represents an ancestor, whose backbone is the painted ridge pole which rests on the main post at the back.

chieftainess had lifted the building *tapu*. The work, particularly the carving, was done under the most sacred *tapu*. Inside, meeting-house walls carried broad slabs upon which tribal ancestors were represented in low relief in highly stylized form. Between these carvings, the walls were lined with horizontal reed-panelling decorated with geometric designs in flax called *tukutuku,* patterns which were echoed in the reed mats that covered the floor. The centre pole supported a relatively realistic likeness, often rendered in the round, of a principal ancestor displaying his tattoos, or *moko*. Rafters and ridge-pole were painted in scroll and spiral designs in red, white and black, an art form native to New Zealand and absent in the rest of Polynesia. On the outside facings of the meeting-house were some of the most striking ancestral figures of all. Carved in deep relief, as Schwimmer has noted, they appeared to confront defiantly the *marae* and the outside world.

Maori wood-carvings were painted with burnt red-ochre mixed with

Right and opposite: Wall slab from the house of Hinematioro, a chieftainess of the Ngati Porou tribe, from Whangara, near Gisborne, dating from the eighteenth century. In New Zealand, as in Polynesia, the female line, especially if it is aristocratic, as in the case of a chieftainess, can be as important as the male line. The small figure between her legs symbolizes the fact that she is the source of future generations, and is an iconographic device which occurs frequently in Maori art.

shark oil. Eyes were represented by inlays of *paua* (abalone) shell. The black and white paints needed for meeting-house rafter designs were made by adding soot or white clay, respectively, to the shark oil. These three colours, ochre-red, black and white, were favoured throughout Polynesia, where they were particularly applied to important canoes.

The 'Kaitaia carving' from the Auckland Museum, which was found in a swamp in Northland, suggests that some kind of carved ceremonial house was a very ancient New Zealand institution. Its style is typically eastern Polynesian/Archaic Maori (the two are virtually indistinguishable), and this indicates that it dates from the Moa Hunter period. The carving may have served as a door-lintel or, more probably, a roof-ridge decoration. Whether the building it originally adorned was some kind of meeting-house or a mortuary structure, we do not know. Certainly it was no simple dwelling place.

The greatest New Zealand carving was not confined to *whare whakairo*. Mortuary buildings, or temporary tombs, where the body of a person of high rank was kept, pending final burial of the bones, were richly carved with ancestral figures – and were highly *tapu*. The beautiful end-pieces of the sacred war-canoes, defiant ancestral warrior figures ever watchful decorated – digging sticks, funnels for feeding highly *tapu* persons, ancestral bones and tribal storehouses – these were part of the very soul of the community; they incorporated the tribe's spiritual *mana*, without which it would perish.

The range of carved objects, however, extended very much further than such community symbols. Every conceivable artifact might be decorated – digging sticks, funnels for feeding highly *tapu* persons, paddles, weapons, boxes for rare feathers, perch-snares, ceremonial adze handles, and almost anything else amenable to the carver's artistry.

Maori social structure, economy, tribal relations and the art forms that gave them symbolic expression were changing and developing continually. The only really clear-cut change in the style of Maori carving (if the luxuriant elaboration of surface decoration which followed the introduction of metal tools is excluded) is that between Archaic Moa Hunter products and those of the Classic Maori. Archaic artifacts are clearly recognizable as Eastern Polynesian in nature, while typically New Zealand designs and motifs dominate the later period. But this is not all. Archaic carvings possess restrained mastery of form with minimal surface patterning. Classic carvings are richly decorated with surface patterns of great vigour. But the surface patterns are never allowed to dominate the form, at any rate in the older pieces. It is hard to be sure, since so few well-dated wooden artifacts have survived from before the eighteenth century, but it is unlikely that over-elaboration ante-dated the *pakeha* (foreign white man's) steel.

Different regional styles did develop, and features characteristic of certain localities can be recognized. The domed head of North Auckland figures and the pointed head favoured in Taranaki can be identified. But often the area of origin of a particular piece, much less who carved it, is not known. One reason for this is that carvers travelled widely. A tentative division into two principal stylistic areas has been made by J. M. McEwen in his innovative article on Maori art. The first contains Northland, Hauraki and part of the Waikato coast and Taranaki; the second, the remaining parts of the North Island, including the notable carving territories of Arawa, Tainui, Matatua, Ngati Porou, Kahungunu, Tawharetoa and Wanganui.

The main motifs in Maori carving are the *tiki* (human form) and the

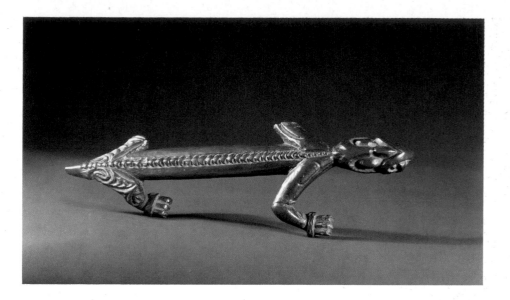

*Opposite above and below: This stone
mauri, made from vesicular lava, was
originally the mauri or soul of Puketapu pa
at Bell Block in North Taranaki. It is a
janus head which looks both ways in
in eternal vigilance.*

*Above right: A carved lizard from the roof
of a storehouse. A lizard is a symbol of
death and of life. It represents spiritual
forces; a lizard placed on any object was all
that was necessary to make that object tapu.*

manaia (bird-man). Subsidiary ones are such *taniwha* (sea monsters) as fish-men, stylized whales and, less commonly, lizards. Of geometric patterns, the double spiral is the most characteristic.

The origin of the word *tiki* dates back to the myth that the first male created by Tane was called 'Tiki'. Thus, when man first carved the human form in wood, he called his creation *tiki*. These human forms nearly always represent ancestors, generally real though sometimes mythological. Even in the most naturalistic carvings the head, being the seat of the greatest *tapu*, is disproportionately large. The mouth is often accentuated and the tongue out-thrust, both to ward off evil and as a gesture of defiance. Facial tattoos or *moko,* an art form in their own right, are meticulously depicted on these *tiki*. The hand is generally shown as three fingered with a rudimentary thumb. The stance, as in Hawaii, Tahiti and Rarotonga is aggressive, the knees slightly flexed. In male figures the penis is erect; female counterparts emphasize the vulva, sometimes with small figures emerging. This epitome of feminine *noa* was functional in the doorways of meeting-houses, where it was thought to drain away any dangerous *tapu* from those crossing the threshold. The little birth figures, like the male phallus, celebrated and invoked the fertility of the tribal forbears.

The 'ear tufts' on some low-relief *tiki* appear to represent the ears of *ruru,* the owl, a bird well known to be the repository of ancestral spirits and the associate of the folk hero Rua, who won the secret of carving from the gods. The big slanted abalone-shell eyes of the more stylized *tiki* are called 'owl eyes' by the East Coast tribes. The typically beaked mouth and the three-fingered hands of stylized *tiki* are notably bird-like.

The purpose and meaning of any particular *tiki* carving, as well as the shape of the structure it embellished, influenced the carver's treatment. Free-standing or high relief images were often carved in the round. They were attached to, or were part of, meeting-house ridge-support poles, or else they surmounted stockades. As meeting-houses increased in size such standing *tiki* were made correspondingly larger. The ancestral figures in low relief on the oblong meeting-house wall-panels were carved with flattened heads to fit the shape of the panels and their eye sockets and brow ridges were slanted upwards to fill out the upper corners of the slabs. The major image was generally flanked by *manaia* (bird-men), spiral designs, lizards, or smaller *tiki,* such as suckling babes or birth figures. Or else an object was added that illustrated some well-known attribute of the ancestor (or ancestress) – a ceremonial adze, a flute or a club perhaps.

While the shape of the wall panels dictated a flattened treatment of *tiki*, it was just the reverse with the elongated forms of *tiki* carved on spear points and on the bow pieces of canoes.

Much controversy centres around *manaia*. Is the *manaia* in fact a bird–man or is it a *tiki* in profile? Barrow supports the first interpretation, Buck and McEwen the second. There does indeed exist a profile form of *tiki* but it does not look like a *manaia*. On the other hand, bird–man motifs do occur in other parts of Polynesia. The case for *manaia* as 'bird-men' seems sound, and in this book it will be taken as such. It has been suggested that *manaia* had something to do with an individual's *mana*, pointing out that '*manaia*' in Hawaiian means 'containing *mana*'. One puzzling feature of *manaia* carvings is that they are often shown as biting human figures, a circumstance not satisfactorily explained.

The whale or *pakake* is commonly rendered with a recognizable cetacian body and tail flukes but with a totally stylized curved or spiral head. The lizard, a creature that used to evoke much fear, is sometimes depicted in *manaia*, *taniwha* or human combination. In other instances it is carved realistically, though adapted to the space available.

A particular variety of the *taniwha* (sea monster) is known as the *marakihau*. This combines features of man and fish, having a human head, three- or four-fingered hands and a body that tapers away into a spiral 'tail', sometimes terminating in a foot. It has an elongated tubular tongue, which is often shown sucking a fish. *Marakihau* were reputed to be able to do the same with canoes, so that sea monsters were, not unnaturally, feared by fishermen and seamen.

The central fragment of a lintel of a chief's house, which was carved in the East Cape region in about 1800. It shows a human figure in the middle, with two manaia at the sides. It is decorated with taratara a kae notches.

The origin of the various spiral designs arouses as much controversy as does that of the bird-men. A strong case exists for postulating some relation between the spiral and the curving fronds of the young fern. Significantly, the pattern is quite unknown in the rest of Polynesia, the only 'example' outside New Zealand being a spiral tattoo on the buttocks of a Marquesan warrior, now known to have been the work of an imaginative nineteenth-century engraver who filled in the blank space on an etching with a Maori design. This limited distribution suggests a New Zealand inspiration for the design's prevalence and elaboration, if not necessarily for its ultimate origin. Buck noted that the pierced double-spiral motif carved on the bow pieces of war canoes are called *pitau* or *tete*, terms which refer primarily to the curling fronds of young ferns. Thus the phrase '*pitau whakarei waka*' means literally 'the fern frond that beautifies the canoe'. Ferns played a very considerable part in Maori life. Bracken root was not only a staple food but was deified as Haumia-tiki-tiki; tree fern trunks were used for building and fencing. The fern could sometimes be a verbal symbol of chieftainship; '*he tete kura*', 'a red fern frond', being a poetic phrase meaning 'chief'. While the words *pitau* and *tete* could have originally referred to the art motif and been only subsequently applied to the plant, the reverse seems more likely. At least forty-five kinds of spiral are used in Maori carving, the greatest elaboration being found in the Auckland, Bay of Plenty and East Coast areas. The double spiral in its various forms is perhaps the most characteristic of all.

While the fern motif seems reasonably well established as one exemplar of the carved spiral, there is no reason to suppose that the rich profusion of spiral designs in Maori art were inspired by only a single group of objects. The mariner's coiled rope, for instance, forms a perfect spiral. *Manaia* forms are often depicted intertwined in Maori spirals, leading one to speculate on the possibility of some kinship with the interlocking bird-beak motifs that are favourites in northern Melanesia. It is also tempting to draw a parallel between the extraordinary persistence of the basic kit of Austronesian maritime technology and the survival of echoes of ancient artistic concepts and modes of expression. Examples of every variety of Austronesian water-craft, from double canoes to reed rafts, are known to have been constructed in New Zealand, where they underwent major modifications in response to local conditions. It seems reasonable to suppose that something similar took place with art motifs in general – not just the spiral.

The rich development of the carver's art which took place in New Zealand was never matched in any other part of Polynesia. To what extent its ultimate well-springs were part of the culture brought to New Zealand by the Eastern Polynesian immigrants cannot be determined. Whatever its origins, the spectacular flowering of the art must be considered a product of the special Maori genius.

The most important question that arises from this brief analysis of the

These two rock drawings from limestone shelters in South Canterbury are executed in charcoal. Both exhibit a sophisticated use of space. In the earlier one (below) of c. 1400, bird-like figures and fish oppose one another. The other, probably from the sixteenth century (below right) shows taniwha, one of whom has swallowed a man and is drowning another.

symbols portrayed by the Maori artist-craftsmen is whether the admitted ambiguities in interpretation necessarily invalidate any conception of the carver's view of his world. Surely not. The general picture is reasonably clear, even if the particular is obscured. One can visualize the *tohunga whakairo*, working under conditions of high *tapu*, giving artistic form and substance to his veneration of the tribal ancestors and depicting them in a spiritual-material continuum, wherein birds, fish, reptiles and human beings partook of one another's attributes in varying degrees. The precise meaning of many of his symbols may be lost forever, but his concept of a world order that combined sacred and profane, mythological and actual in a single all-embracing unity is vividly conveyed by his art.

One last point. Maori traditional wood-carving is a vital and expanding art form today. This very vitality, with the continual change and development that accompanies it, tends to obscure past traditions with newly budding concepts. This may be a matter of regret to the purist art historian; it can only delight those who prefer a vibrant, living culture to the closed book of the past.

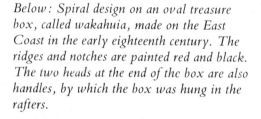

KAHU KURA AND TIKI

Feather Cloak and Pendant

It is unfortunate that no clothing which definitely dates from the Archaic, or Moa Hunter, period has survived. The most reliable data on pre-European-contact Maori clothing, ornaments and tattoos, come from the first of the European visitors: Abel Tasman in 1642, Cook in 1769, 1772 and 1778, de Surville in 1769, the ill-fated Marion du Fresne in 1772 and Governor King of New South Wales in 1793. The explorers' observations are amplified by archaeological findings, and by traditions and chants.

Archaic-phase Maori clothing evolved in response to the relatively harsh New Zealand climate that greeted the immigrants. The typical clothes of the high islands of tropical Polynesia were made from bark cloth (*tapa*) beaten from the inner bark of the paper mulberry. Although the Eastern Polynesian settlers in New Zealand were successful introducing the paper mulberry into North Auckland, it did not flourish. Banks, the naturalist on the *Endeavour,* saw a small stand of trees in the Bay of Islands in 1769 that was carefully cultivated and protected. He wrote perceptively:

> After this they showed as a great rarity 6 plants of what they called *Aouta* from whence they made cloth like the Otahite cloth; the plant proved exactly the same, as the name is the same as is used in the islands . . . Whether the Climate does not well agree with it I do not know, but they seemed to value it very much and that it was scarce among them I am inclined to believe, as we have not seen among them pieces large enough for any use but sticking into the holes of their Ears.

It is interesting that despite their isolation in New Zealand for so many centuries, there were in 1769 still some Maori who knew the technology associated with manufacturing bark cloth. The failure of the paper mulberry to flourish even in the warmer northern parts of New Zealand meant that some substitute material had to be found. The one chosen was New Zealand flax. And so a new technology for manufacturing flax garments gradually evolved, and a new assortment of clothing was produced. Decorative elements were drawn from other plants and animals of the environment, and these gave New Zealand work a distinctive local aspect.

Although no Moa Hunter age clothing exists today, changes in style can be noted from contemporary accounts and archaeological discoveries. Ear-plugs, for instance, were not seen by any of the eighteenth-century explorers, and so had presumably dropped out of fashion. But carvers,

A kiwi-feather cloak decorated with a taniko (tapestry) border, said to have been made by the Maori of the West Coast of the South Island in 1863. Kiwi-feather cloaks replaced the earlier dogskin cloaks as being the most prestigious of all. Kiwi feathers were always prized, especially albino ones such as these. There are 114 rows of stiches locking the warp in place and also tying the quills of the feathers in place. The flax fibre lining is soft. Natural dyes have been used for the border.

particularly on the East Coast, continued to portray them, as evidenced by a meeting-house gable mask obtained by Cook's officers. Archaic Maori 'assemblages' included necklaces made up of bone spools or reels, seal ivory pendants in the form of whale teeth and chevroned amulets. When the Classic Maori life-style superseded the Archaic, these were replaced by greenstone *hei tiki* (human form) and *rei puta* pendants. (The latter were pendants made from whales' teeth). A more gradual change in style is apparent in the 300 sixteenth-century combs excavated from a swamp at Kauri Point in the Bay of Plenty, which illustrate the transition from the square to the more rounded forms that were still being worn in the late eighteenth century. Except for the Archaic to Classic phase transition, and the still earlier adaptations that followed initial settlement, men's styles and fashions altered at a very leisurely pace.

It was as a result of the poor showing of the tropical paper mulberry (*aute*) that New Zealand flax became the primary raw material for clothing. Although it was supplemented by cabbage-tree leaves, rushes, dogskin and dog fur, feathers and human hair, the techniques for preparing flax fibre and its weaving (*whatu*) were the real basis of Maori clothing manufacture. As in many other cultures, this was an industry in which the work was done by women.

A few cloaks and loincloths of plaited flax that have survived from the Chatham Islands (where Archaic styles persisted) suggest that the first New Zealand garments may have been similarly fine-plaited – but they would have been inordinately stiff. At any rate, the technology by Classic times involved scraping off the outer layers, twisting the fibres into thread, and finger-weaving them from a frame of two weaving sticks or pegs stuck into the ground.

Above and right: Stone pounder, which has a human head on the butt and chevrons at the mid-point representing arms. Stone pounders were used for softening flax fibre for weaving cloaks. In prehistoric times, Taranaki was famous all over New Zealand for the fineness and beauty of its cloaks. The local importance of cloak production and the resulting technology has been combined with the stone sculpture tradition to produce this pounder. Found at New Plymouth, c. 1850, it is made from local volcanic andesite.

First came the extraction of the fibre from the flax leaf, a process known as *haaro*, that was well described by Governor King in 1793. He recounted that the female operators removed with their nails the centre and edges of the leaf, leaving strips 2 centimetres ($\frac{3}{4}$ inch) wide and 1 metre (3 feet) long. The outer green covering of the leaves was next stripped away, from the upper and lower surfaces in turn, with the sharp edge of a mussel shell. The resulting strips of fibre could be used as they were for fishing lines and nets, but for clothing the fibres had to be well beaten in a stream to soften them, and the impurities had to be teased out with mussel shells. Then, after drying, the fibres were twisted into single-ply threads that were sometimes doubled.

For the single-pair twined technique a series of warps (vertical threads) were made by doubling a long weft (horizontal) thread – cut to the required measure – round the first warp at the upper end and making a half-turn to enclose it before taking in successive warps with a similar half turn of the two weft threads. When the full width of the warp was completed the weft threads were tied together with a reef knot. To hang the set of warps between two weaving sticks stuck in the ground, separate threads were tied to each end of the weft row and then to the upper ends of the sticks so that the row was held taut with the warps hanging down vertically. The space between the weft rows remained the same within a specific length of weaving, but the extent of the space varied with the type of garment being woven. The subsequent weft rows were worked in the same way but not attached to the weaving sticks. When the worked material reached ground level, the bottom weft row was either hitched to the upper ends of the original weaving sticks, or attached to a second pair, and additional weft rows were then added as required.

To distinguish the technique from conventional loom-weaving, the term 'finger-weaving' is used to denote the process of manipulating the weft pair round each vertical warp, and 'downward-weaving' for the process as it evolved from the rows of finger-weaving.

Rain capes were the first garments to be made with this single-pair twine; these had overlapping tags of flax on the outside which served to shed the rain 'like a shingled roof'. A more elaborate two-pair weft technique was used for some of the better cloaks (though not for the

Above: Chevron pendant, made in one piece from a sperm-whale tooth. A beautiful parrot shape is at the top of the chevron line. At the sides are hand and foot projections. The pendant was hung from perforations at the top behind the bird's tail. Found at Okains Bay, Banks Peninsula, it probably dates to about the fourteenth century, and is usually regarded as Archaic.

prestigious dogskin ones). The weaving of geometrically patterned borders, called *taniko*, was considered to be the ultimate in Maori weaving. *Taniko* colours were predominantly black and brown, with colours being added increasingly after about 1750. Highly elaborate garments, such as the dogskin cloak with its intricate black and white *taniko* border which was collected on Cook's first voyage, were probably never matched by later work, which was much simpler.

There was no such thing as a Maori technology divorced from ritual and spiritual connotations. Weaving was no exception. Girls were ritually dedicated to the craft when they were eight days old and subsequently underwent years of practical instruction from their female relatives. The most accomplished girls would be individually initiated by a priestly *tohunga* at a special ceremony.

The initial dedication of baby girls was part of their baptism. The child was named, sprinkled with water from a stream and her umbilical cord was severed. The accompanying invocation was addressed, not to the baby but to the umbilical cord:

Seek food for yourself, umbilical cord!
Go for firewood for yourself, umbilical cord!
Weave garments for yourself, umbilical cord!

(from Mead, 'Imagery, Symbolism and Social Values in Maori Chants' in the *Journal of the Polynesian Society*, 78:3)

Years later, teenagers of special aptitude were initiated into the weaver's 'guild' (*whare pora*) by a priest. *Tohunga* and aspirant weaver were alone in the house. The weaver was seated before two weaving pegs, and the first weft thread was tied across the two weaving pegs. The warp threads were doubled over the weft and the aspirant was ready to weave the first row of single pair (or two-pair interlocking) twine. But before she did so the *tohunga* recited this spell:

Stick in the peg; it is the peg,
Of eager desire, of swiftness.
Stand medium of authority, stand medium of the house,
Send here the weft to be hastily woven
So it may be woven quickly to be soon completed,
. . . . .
Tremble the hill,
The hill leaped up, the mound gathered together;
Heaped up to the sky,
Widely across the land.
Be completed! Be completed!

(from Mead, 'Imagery . . . in Maori Chants')

When the spell was completed the weaver bent forward and bit the sacred peg to 'swallow' the spell, the stomach being the seat of feeling. Having received a ritual blessing, she proceeded to weave the sacred weft, *te aho tapu*. The ceremony was to give the weaver *mana* rather than help as regards instruction. A second part of the ceremony removed the *tapu* from the weaver so she could once more mingle with others. During this, she ate a piece of sour thistle while the final spell was recited.

Clothes and decorations worn by the Maori varied according to sex, rank and occasion. Banks said the minimum requirements for men were:

Right: A korowai, or tag cloak, made by finger-weaving, of fine flax fibre, and decorated with black tags which were in fact lengths of rolled fibre about six inches long, died black and attached at regular intervals. This was a fairly common type of cloak in the early nineteenth century.

Left: Weaving peg from Taranaki. The faces carved on it have paua-shell insets for eyes. Finger-weaving was set up on two pegs, with the lowest weft thread between them. On this thread were hung the warp threads, the other weft lines being added by the fingers while the warp threads were held tight with the toes. No other extra pieces were required, just the two pegs and the fibre.

short beards; hair tied into a knot on top of the head; a decorative comb thrust into the hair beside the topknot; two or three white feathers pushed into the topknot itself; a belt round the waist; and a string from the belt to the penis. This last, the penis girdle (*tuu ure*), was the essential item of male clothing and was described by Cook as '. . . a belt round the waste to which is generally fasten'd a small string which tyes round the Prepuce'. The string served to hold the penis upright for, unlike the female vulva, the male organ was exposed and maintained in an erect position in token of manhood and valour. (Certain war dances derided an opponent for having a drooping penis, which betokened a lack of courage.) Cook remarked that hundreds of men had come dressed thus scantily to see the *Endeavor,* but added that they generally had their other clothing in the canoe to put on 'if it rain'd etc.'.

High fashion in eighteenth century New Zealand, as in eighteenth-century England, was the prerogative of men of rank. Sidney Mead, in his *Traditional Maori Clothing* makes some pertinent observations about chiefly style and fashion:

A fictitious aura of grandeur was achieved by the costume which

increased the size of the body . . . When they dressed up, chiefs were emphasizing their height and body size and at the same time were achieving some added dignity and grandeur with which to impress men and women of chiefly families.

Colours favoured during this period were sharply contrasting – dark blacks and brown contrasting with white. The use of red in garments does not appear to have been widespread at this time, but they did smear themselves with red ochre. Several costumes were all black, for instance some dogskin cloaks . . . All told, the emotional aura of the costume as affected by colour was 'the dark primitive and mysterious look' with glaring contrasts in white.

A particularly revealing pointer to an old-time Maori chief's own attitude is the 'Song by Te Ranginui, for being without a cloak'. He composed this derisive song because a man named Te Moko had publicly shamed him by commenting upon his torn cloak. The words suggest that he tried to exchange the damaged garment with a travelling trader, Rangitapuarewa, but without success. (Te Mui is another name for Te Ranginui himself.)

Eat, oh head lice!
Eat, oh flea!
Eat, oh insect!
Pearce the sleepy-head there!
Paeroa has heard from the wind to the north,
Perhaps Te Mui will not own a red-painted cloak of his own,
To satisfy this man Te Moko;
He said in my direction, 'The dogskin cloak is torn!'
Rangitapuerawa returns empty-handed,
The carrier of prized goods.
Carry this fellow to Whakanau,
To the fluids of dogfish fat
Which will refresh my skin,
Apply the red pigment to my body!

(from Mead, *Traditional Maori Clothing*)

A plain all-purpose garment of high-quality, dressed and bleached flax fibre was very soft and suitable for weaving next to the skin. It might be worn round the shoulders as a cape or cloak or round the waist, or wrapped round the whole body in the form of a kilt, breech-clout or loincloth passed between the legs and tied round the waist with a flax belt. There was little or no decoration on it. This kind of high-quality cloth appears to have been worn by chiefs, old men and women of rank.

Rain capes were made of various materials such as dogskin, cabbage-tree leaves and rushes, as well as flax. All were 'thatched' like sailors' thrum mats. The garments varied from coarse and crude to a highly prized type called a *kahu toi*, and were worn by both sexes. Monkhouse, on Cook's first voyage, gives an excellent description of these garments, which were '. . . coarsely beat out of a kind of narrow Sedge or coarse grass . . . the ends of the stuff about a foot long were left out so as to form

Swamp in the extreme north of the North Island. Swamps like this yield most of the archaic wood sculpture which has been found. It has either sunk or been dumped there to save it from plundering raids, or later perhaps from missionaries.

87

An eighteenth-century wooden hair comb, which would have been worn in a man's topknot. These were often painted with red ochre. This comb, an unusually small and finely carved one, is reproduced in its actual size.

a thick covering layer over layer, and very much what seamen call thrum-Matts . . . some were tied round the neck and some round the loins. Some were so long as to reach down to the knees and secured round the loins with a girdle of matting.'

Dogskin cloaks greatly impressed the early explorers, as they were worn by the principal men who visited their ships and were obviously much valued. Banks wrote, '. . . the great pride of their dress seems to consist in dogs fur, which they use so sparing that to avoid waste they cut into long strips and sew them at a distance from each other upon their Cloth, varying often the colours prettily enough.' The foundation of the cloaks was flax fibre woven with a close single-pair twine. The dog hides were usually cut into strips and oversewn onto this flax fibre foundation. Geometrically patterned *taniko* (borders) usually accompanied the dogskin as decoration. Only rarely were whole skins used as the native dog (*kuri*) was becoming very scarce in late Classic times and was shortly to become extinct. Du Fresne in 1772 stated that the cloaks of chiefs were usually made of dogskin 'which gives them a great advantage when they use it to ward off spears'. These cloaks would be soaked in water before battle, to stiffen them.

Several ornamental cloaks, with plain bodies and edges trimmed with tufts of hair or feathers, were carried back to England. The flax thread was always exceptionally finely prepared and woven either by close single-pair twining or with a spaced two-pair weft; the usual description by the visitors was 'silky'.

Feather cloaks were uncommon at the time of European contact. The most striking was a type called *kahu kura,* of which the artist, Parkinson, wrote in 1769, 'One man in particular, who seemed to be a chief, was painted red, and had on a red garment.' This may have been Banks's chief 'who had an entire dress of the red feathers of parrots'. Feather cloaks made by sewing wood-hen or parakeet skin together, probably dating from the Archaic culture, have been found in Otago burial caves. Magnificent feather cloaks have been preserved in Hawaii, so the New Zealand examples could be extensions of the Eastern Polynesian tradition.

Korowai cloaks are known in the early period only from a painting by Parkinson. These were full-length cloaks or fine-quality flax fibre, the body of which was decorated with lengths of rolled fibre dyed black and attached at regular intervals. The black hanging 'thrums' were about 15 centimetres (6 inches) long and constituted the only decoration on the body of the cloak, though there was usually a heavy black fringe at the lower border.

The number of feathers worn by warriors in their topknots seems to have increased with the passage of time. Only a single feather was sported by those seen by Tasman in 1642: '. . . they wore tufts of black hair upon the top of their heads and tied fast in the manner of the Japanese . . . surmounted by a large thick white feather'. In 1773, Parkinson depicted topknots adorned with three white feathers and a comb. Crozet (who accompanied du Fresne and after whom the Islands were named) was in the Bay of Islands the previous year and stated that 'Only those amongst the fighting men who have committed acts of ferocity or treason have the right to wear four plumes in their hair.'

To complete his ensemble, the warrior wore white feathers or greenstone ear pendants suspended from each ear and a whale-tooth or greenstone pendant round the neck. Facial and body (mostly buttocks) tattoo was essential, and was most profuse on the older, highly respected war leaders. The warrior also carried a weapon in his right hand.

The hair was often rubbed with shark oil and powdered with red

Kahu topuni, a chief's war cloak. It has a closely woven back decorated with thin strips of skin from the kuri, the dog originally brought to New Zealand by Maori forebears. This cloak was a peace offering given by the Arawa tribes to the Ngaiterangi tribe of Tauranga at the conclusion of a long and bloody war which culminated in the battle of Te Tumu near Maketu in the year 1836.

ochre. Sometimes the women also followed this custom. Ear-lobes were pierced and decorated with parents' teeth, white feathers, abalone shell, pieces of bone, worked fish-teeth, or greenstone pendants and spiral ornaments. Bracelets and shell anklets were worn on occasion. Necklaces would be of black stones of berries, teeth, feather bundles and perfumed leaves, birdskin and feathers, greenstone *tiki* or *rei puta*.

Human form ornaments, *tiki*, were probably adaptations of wood-carvings, first in bone, later in greenstone. The earlier examples are mostly upright, the later ones having the head inclined towards one shoulder. The upright type closely conforms to the treatment of the human figure in wood-carving but must have involved much labour to reproduce in bone or hard stone; the second type would have been easier to shape.

To distinguish them from the massive wooden figures, pendant *tikis* were termed *hei tiki* (*hei* meaning to suspend). When sex was indicated in a *tiki* it was always female, so identification with Tane's male organ seems unlikely. Some experts feel that identification of *tiki* with the foetus was also a rationalization, though a pre-European one, of an object whose configuration had been influenced by the material from which it was made. There is also some scepticism about the supposed fertility stimulating role of the ornament, *tiki* being worn by men as often as by women.

For women, the minimal clothing consistent with modesty was an apron-girdle (a type of *maro*) to cover the pubis, it being considered highly immodest to expose the pubic region in any way (except as a mortal insult – as in expressing contempt for enemy warriors).

Women's clothing was drab. According to Cook's party their dress was less 'affected' than men's, and their hair was generally cut short. They were 'more covered' than men though rarely with 'fine clothes'. Women too wore capes as cloaks or kilts, leaving the breasts uncovered, and sometimes a skirt, with a piece of bark cloth draped round the shoulders as protection against the cool of the evening.

The invariably worn apron-girdle was generally coarse-fibred and utilitarian, though high-status women on formal occasions sported aprons decorated with red feathers or strips of dogskin. The apron itself consisted of a plaited cord with a bunch or fringe of leaves over the pubic area. Associated with the apron were perfumes. The waist-cord was plaited of *kaaretu* leaves which smelt rather like vanilla. The fringe of leaves was of some aromatic plant like *raukawa*. (*Raukawa* scent was the perfume used by the celebrated chieftainess Mahinaarangi when she was being courted by the Waikato chief, Tuurongo, early in the sixteenth

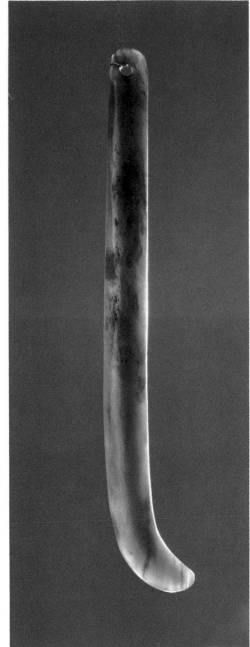

Two greenstone ornaments. The ear pendant (above) was worn singly by a male. It dates to before European contact, and is probably from the East Coast of the South Island. The heitiki (left) was made in the eighteenth century in the Northland, and given as a gift to a missionary. Heitikis, especially greenstone ones, were charged with and accumulated mana by being worn by either male or female chiefs who emanated mana. These heitikis also gained mana through being given to people who possessed mana – that is, they were given into the safekeeping of people who were considered to be of exceptional moral integrity (in this case, a missionary). It was always recorded where a tiki of mana came from, and it was supposed eventually to be

returned to its original keepers. When the Europeans came, they carried away the heitikis forever, and the continuity of mana was thus broken. This illustrates the Maori attitude to property generally. In their relationship to things, the Maori were far less materialistic than their European counterparts, and never saw possession as being personal. It was the mana of an object that determined its value, rather than its intrinsic meaning or its beauty.

Above right: This kaitaka was a prestige cloak made in the Taranaki area in the early nineteenth century. The beauty of this type of cloak lies in the softness and silky sheen of the beaten flax fibre from which is was made. The tapestry base serves as a weight to pull the cloak into shape when worn. The Maori stopped making these cloaks in about 1835.

Below: Woman's rapaki, or skirt, bordered with taniko weaving in Taranaki style. This garment, worn by high-ranking women on special occasions, incorporates some imported wool and dates to the second quarter of the nineteenth century.

century. They named their son Raukawa and he founded a tribe called the People of Raukawa – *Ngati Raukawa*.)

Auxiliary items of clothing included belts, which were used to hold up kilts or sometimes worn outside cloaks and were the same for both sexes. There were no head-dresses for men aside from the requisite combs and feathers. Women sometimes wore chaplets or head-bands, often made from scented leaves. The only other kind of 'hat' was a widow's mourning cap which was frequently decorated with feathers or the heads of birds. While in some parts of New Zealand women's hair was cut short and undecorated, in other regions older women had theirs tied on top of their heads, sometimes in a topknot which might be adorned with the feathers of forest birds, leaving the feathers of sea-birds for males. Unmarried girls wore their hair down. The face itself was often painted, usually with red ochre in shark oil, and tattoos for both sexes completed the body and facial decoration of the pre-European-contact Maori.

The symmetry of the face dominates face and head design. Facial tattoo patterns which follow a curvilinear style of ornamentation are symmetrical, the ear ornaments similarly balance, the topknot is centred on the top of the head and the feathers fit into the overall pattern . . . The overall effect of this design is to give a dignified air to the face and head and at the same time to draw attention to that part of the body. An even more awe-inspiring effect was achieved by the very black facial tattoo which gave a 'dark' appearance to the countenance.

(Mead, *Traditional Maori Clothing*)

Maori tattooing differed fundamentally from the needle-puncture method used in the rest of Polynesia, and in contemporary Western tattooing, where the full thickness of the skin is not penetrated and blood is not drawn. The Maori art of chisel *moko* was virtually 'skin-carving' and almost, as has been suggested, a direct derivation from wood-carving. There are the same curves and double spirals and it would seem that experiments were made on wood before working on the more sensitive human skin. The main lines of the design were deeply sunken so that

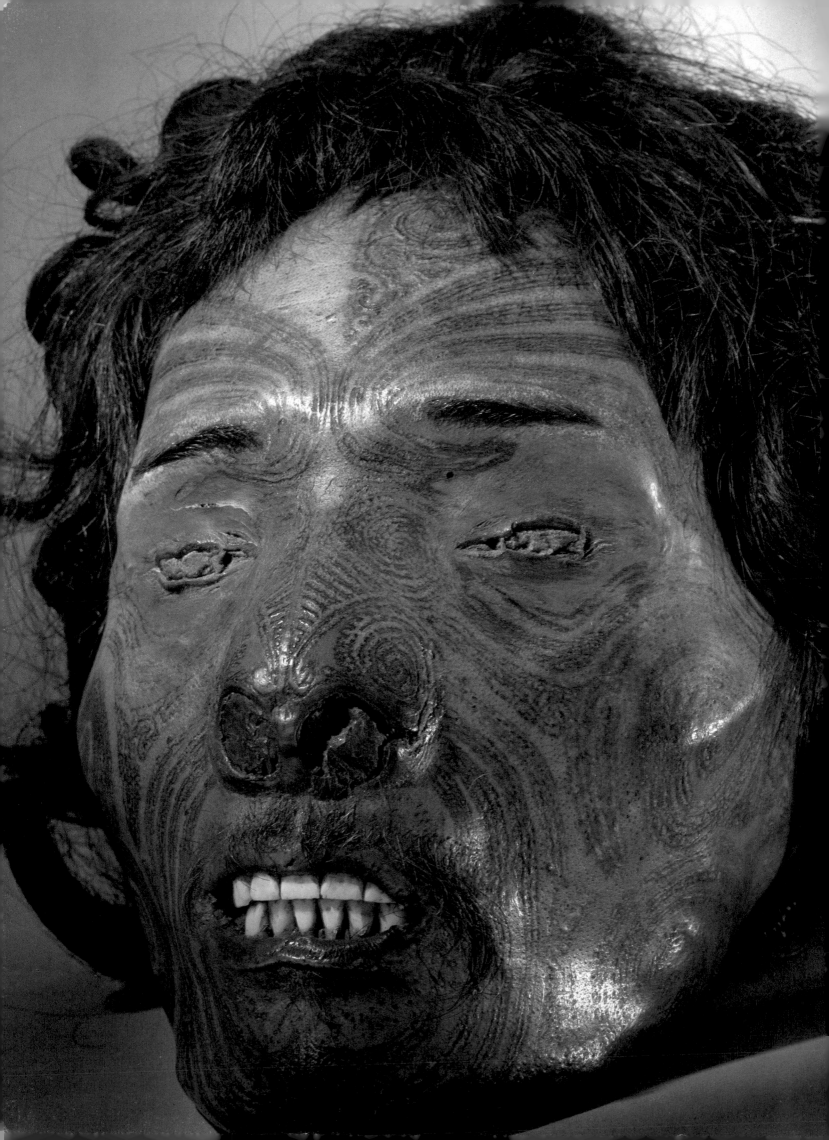

the spaces between parallel lines stood out as ridges, very like designs on wood.

When you look at the main Maori tattooing instrument the influence of wood-carving becomes more than ever apparent, for it is nothing less than a small, hafted adze. With such implements the tattooer, tapping with a mallet, cut through the skin instead of puncturing it and, by continued application of the narrow cutting-blade, had more control in forming his incised design than if he had used a knife-like instrument. Toothed chisels were used for filling-in and pecking-in the dye during the operation. *Moko* was a long and painful process during which the operative part, especially the face, became swollen so that the subject had to be fed through a special funnel. The copious flow of blood was wiped away with flax-fibre swabs. The whole operation took months; in fact it was usual to add tattoos year after year as the individual increased in wealth and prestige as a warrior. The dye was made from the resin of the kauri pine or the totara conifer, which was then burnt to yield a bluish-black soot. Mixed with pigeon fat, the soot was kept in ornamented pummice containers.

Men were tattooed not only on the face, but also on the thighs and buttocks. This distribution of the tattooed area was common to other parts of Polynesia but the spiral designs were uniquely Maori. The facial tattoo of women was more modest, being confined to the chin and lips. So painful was the process that some women could not face the ordeal of having the upper lip tattooed after the lower lip and chin had healed, and they suffered a good deal of shame thereafter. Some women, on the other hand, had their thighs and breasts tattooed in addition to their lips and chin. *Moko* was a highly skilled operation carried out by experts (*tohunga ta moko*) who travelled the country to execute commissions exactly like the greatest wood-carvers. Their reward in gift-exchange was correspondingly high.

It seems that only the older men could afford to have full facial tattoos. Neither du Fresne's nor Cook's companions, nor Governor King a little later, ever mentioned fully tattooed young men. In fact, Crozet states categorically that only distinguished warriors had the right 'to tatu the skin of the face, their buttocks and the hands, and which is considered amongst them as the highest distinction. There is no doubt that in order to arrive at the pre-eminence of such complete tatuing a man must have killed and eaten many of his fellows.'

When tattooed men died, their heads were often preserved and kept in their families. Thus when important chiefs were killed in distant battles, their preserved heads were brought back to be wept over by the widow and the other members of the tribe. The heads of detested enemy chiefs were also brought back to the *pa,* in order that they might be reviled and insulted, especially by the widows and orphans for whose plight they were responsible.

In Maori facial tattooing, a combination of various motifs was assigned to particular parts, each motif having a special name. Nevertheless, *moko* was different for each person and a mark of identity for the owner. It emphasized the sacredness of man. During the time of carving, the patient was strictly *tapu*. He was fed through a funnel, not only because of the swollen tissues, but to avoid his *tapu* being profaned by his lips touching cooked food. The tattoo was certainly not considered to be merely a decoration to conceal the real face – indeed a Maori of rank did not get his real face until he was tattooed; thenceforth the tribal self engraved upon him became his permanent mask whose bold convolutions expressed the tribal spirit.

Opposite: A dried, tattooed head, dating to about 1820, from the West Coast of the North Island, probably taken by northern Ngapuhi raiders who, after they obtained guns, became the scourge of other tribes. European traders demanded two such heads, a ton of potatoes or a shipload of dressed flax fibre for one musket. This led to a trade in heads, and slaves were tattooed and killed specifically for the European market. The practice of drying heads was an ancient one, but had formerly been confined to enemies against whom there was a particular grudge, or to revered chiefs, whose heads, if they were killed away from home, would be dried and taken home for the funeral.

Above: A carved hardwood mask with pierced eyes and mouth showing moko patterns similar to those known from dried heads. These patterns were highly personal, and would identify the person represented.

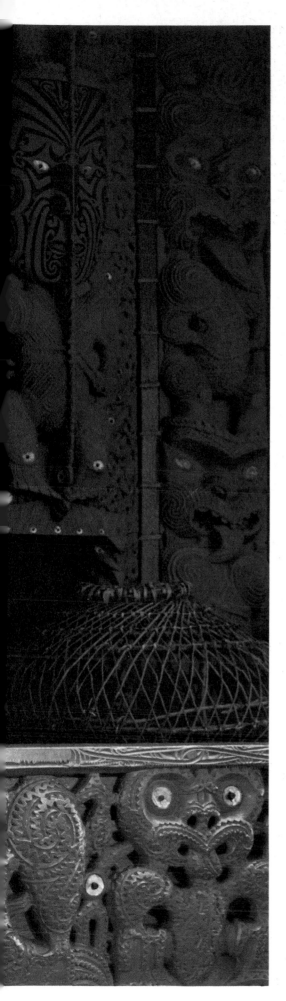

TE WAIATA
Song, Dance, Games

The Maori were, and indeed are, extremely creative people. Even their games showed artistry, and their music and dance were expressive of a wide range of moods. Maori oratory, with its frequent reference to the mythic past, was (and still is) a highly developed art, in its subtlety and splendour reminiscent of the oratory of Ancient Greece. Maori poetry, ranging from sublime pathos to rowdy humour, is some of the most evocative ever composed.

It is not always easy to distinguish between children's and adult's pastimes in old New Zealand. For instance, young boys threw reed 'spears' at one another as an enjoyable game, but it was also essential training for battle. Moreover, some games were played by people of all ages.

Skipping over a rope swung by companions was as popular in New Zealand as it is with children elsewhere. So was anything to do with water. Boys and girls learned to swim early, sometimes assisted by gourd floats. Side-stroke, breast-stoke, overarm and back-stroke were all used. Dives were always made feet first. Body-surfing with or without small boards was a pastime for young people on suitable coasts. Toboganning was largely a children's pastime, using *ti kouka* leaves or wooden toboggans.

While rolling supplejack hoops was a favourite occupation of boys and girls, adults, as a mark of derision, played with hoops decorated with the tattooed skin of slain opponents. On every high river bank near a village a single vine suspended from a branch overhanging the water served as an ever-popular swing for boys and girls, the outswing terminating in a feet-first plunge into the water. An adult equivalent was the giant swing *morere,* which was a tall, slanted pole erected near a river bank with a number of liana ropes attached to the top. The players swung out on the ropes and dropped off into the water feet-first. Spinning tops was another game not limited to children. There were two varieties, whip tops and humming tops. Whip tops resembled European ones in shape but were rather larger, especially those used by adults. The favourite material was matai wood; the whip was a leash of flax cords tied to an eighteen-inch stick. The humming top was similar except for an upper shaft which produced the sound. Walking on stilts tended to be a young men's sport, especially when it involved wrestling. Kites, called *manu tukutuku* ('bird on a cord being paid out'), were flown for sport, but for the more serious purpose of divination, *tohunga* flew special priests' kites

Carving of an embracing couple in the Te Puawai O Te Arawa storehouse.

termed *manu whara*. A popular entertainment was provided by *karetao* puppets or jumping jacks, of which the arms were manipulated by strings to the accompaniment of a chant.

Cat's cradle string figure-making (*whai*) is a world-wide occupation. In New Zealand, a six-foot looped cord was stretched between the hands and the more complicated figures were made with the aid of the teeth and toes. The figures were given names, many of which represented incidents or characters in mythology. The most expert exponents of the craft were generally women.

A peculiarly New Zealand game which vaguely resembles draughts was *mu torere*. The board, made of wood or bark, was likened to the eight tentacles of an octopus; the 'draught' pieces were coloured or marked pebbles, and there were two players.

Games of strength and quickness such as running races, long-jump competitions and wrestling, tended to shade into military training. Canoe-racing was a sport for both sexes, especially obstacle racing, but racing between the huge war canoes was a sport for warriors. Dart-throwing for boys began with reeds or fern stems and progressed to 1.8 metre (6 foot) blunted manuka shafts. The recipient would learn to parry, side-step or catch the spear in his left hand. Darts were bounced off a special mound in competition, or else jerked forward by a cord attached to a throwing-stick. In the latter form, darts were used in war as firesticks to set fire to enemy thatched houses.

Jackstones or knuckle bones was a game of dexterity. It was played with five pebbles, the movements being in ordered, named sequence. One movement, for instance, consisted in throwing up all five pebbles and catching as many as possible on the back of the hand. When a player missed a movement an opponent took over. The winner was the one who completed the most sequences.

A particularly popular game of skill was the stick game, *ti rakau*. The players knelt in a circle with two sticks each. In time to a chant, they beat the sticks together and then threw first one and then the other to the neighbour on the right, the sticks being thrown in a vertical position. Each threw the first stick with the right hand and caught the incoming stick with the same, now empty, hand, then threw the second stick with the left hand and with it caught the incoming stick. This continued for some beats, then the two sticks were beaten together and the tempo quickened. Those who dropped the stick fell out until the last one left became the winner. Though both sexes participated in *ti rakau* its relevance to catching spears is obvious. Similar to the stick game was *ti ringa*, which was played with hands without sticks. The players stood facing each other and, in time to a chant, they executed quick movements to each beat. Failure to anticipate and match each successive movement meant loss of points.

Musical instruments were many and various. Percussion instruments comprised the gong, castanets and the Jew's harp. Rather surprisingly, the shark-skin drum of tropical Polynesia was not retained in New Zealand.

The most spectacular percussion instrument was the *pahu* (war gong). George French Angas, a young Australian artist who visited New Zealand in 1846, described a *pahu* as 'an oblong piece of wood, about six feet long, with a groove in the centre; and being slung by ropes of flax, was struck with a heavy piece of wood, by a man who sat on an elevated scaffold, crying out at every stoke the watchword of alarm'. The call to arms of the sentry and the boom of the great gong must have been awe-inspiring in the extreme to people who lived always in the shadow of violence. Another variety of *pahu*, used by forest tribes like the Tuhoe, was a long down-pointing tongue adzed out from a still-standing hollow tree.

Castanets (*tokere*) were made of wood or bone and were used, a pair in each hand. The *pakuru* (Jew's harp) was a wooden strip, eighteen inches long, which was held between the teeth. The end not held in the teeth was vibrated by being tapped with a stick in time to the words of a song. The *roria* was a simpler version made of supplejack, and its end was flicked with a finger.

The two classes of Maori wind instruments were trumpets and flutes. There were four varieties of trumpet, or *pu*, the simplest being a flax instrument, generally a child's toy, but sometimes used as a makeshift trumpet to announce the approach to a village. The triton-shell trumpets, which were sometimes ornamented with dogskin or feathers, had carved wooden mouthpieces about six inches long. Among their other functions, they were blown to announce the birth of a chief's son. The long wooden war trumpets (*pu kaea*) were used to sound the alarm against attack and were carried by war parties on major campaigns. The fourth kind of trumpet was the *pu torino*. It was blown from one end and the hole for the emission of the sound was in the middle, carved to represent a mouth in a stylized face. The mouthpiece was also carved with *tiki* or *manaia* motifs.

The Maori flutes, *koauau*, *porutu*, *whio* and *nguru* (this last is sometimes termed a whistle) differed according to their length and thickness and whether the distal end was open or closed, but every variety had three finger holes or stops. *Koauau* were most highly esteemed and upon them was lavished the most elaborate carving when they were made of wood. Bone instruments were more simply carved, but were considered more valuable, since the raw material had usually been obtained from an enemy slain in battle. But the reputation of the *koauau* rested not so much on its warlike connotations as on its seductive power. Women were reputed to be particularly susceptible to its message and it is said that prudent husbands watched their wives with especial care lest they be entranced by the beguiling notes of a handsome musician.

One of the most famous of all Maori love stories centres round the *koauau* flute-playing young *rangatira* Tutanekai and the high-born maiden Hinemoa. Tutanekai lived on Mokoia Island in Lake Rotorua, where, of an evening, he used to play on his flute. The sound of the music could be heard across the lake at Owhata and it charmed the beautiful Hinemoa, who lived there. When Tutanekai visited the mainland with his *hapu* (clan), he and Hinemoa met and fell in love. The young man had to return to his island, but the lovers arranged that every night he would play and that Hinemoa would follow the sound of his music and join him. Tutanekai kept up a nightly serenade but Hinemoa, being a chief's daughter, had been reserved for a political marriage and her people, suspecting something was afoot, hid all the canoes. Undeterred, the maiden selected six large dry gourds as floats and set out to swim to the island, more than a mile away, guided by the notes of the *koauau*. The brave girl landed exhausted by the hot spring Waikimihia, where she rested and refreshed herself, and it was there that Tutanekai found her. So impressed were the Arawa at Hinemoa's courage that they withdrew all objections to the match.

There were many kinds of dances, or *haka*, serving different functions. The war *haka*, *peruperu*, was performed before battle as a prelude to hand-to-hand combat. The leader held a short club (*patu*), and his follow-

This pahu, or war gong, was fashioned from a hollow tree to leave a suspended tongue which was struck. It is decorated with a male figure, whose head is missing, clasping a female child.

ers held long blade clubs (*taiaha*) obliquely in their right hands, which they moved up and down to the stamp of their right feet. In the following typical *peruperu* the first movements were measured and stately, but from '*kia rere*' onwards the action became frenzied; eyes rolling, tongues protruding, the warriors leapt and thudded down in wild abandon, but in perfect time to the roar of the chant.

> *Close in!*
> *Ah, ah.*
> *Open out!*
> *Ah, ah.*
> *Let the seal fly away*
> *to the distance,*
> *And there gaze fearfully back!*
> *Ah, ah, it is war.*

(from B. Mitcalfe, *Maori Poetry*)

The 'seal' refers to the fleeing enemy.

The ordinary *haka, taparahi,* danced on a wide variety of occasions, lacked both the terrifying ferocity of the war dance and its sacred dedication to bloodshed and the god of war. It was a wild dance nevertheless, with much leaping, head-rolling and thigh-slapping in time to solo lead and chorus, but no weapons were carried and women often participated. Depending on the occasion, a *haka* could have humorous passages (during an entertainment on the home *marae*), or be formal, as when welcoming distinguished guests from another *hapu* or tribe, or it could be danced to a sad lament at a mourning *tangi*.

· The most beautiful Maori dance was the softly rhythmical *poi* dance of the women. It was the complete antithesis of the violently masculine *peruperu*. The *poi* (ball) is native to New Zealand. In Classic times the slightly elongated ball about the size of an orange was made of close flax netting or a woven cloth stuffed with dried *raupo* (rushes). *Poi* were usually decorated with tufts of dog's hair and attached to a string. The string was longer than is customary today and the movements slower. The dancer looped the string over the forefinger of the right hand and, as she swayed to the rhythm of the dance, the *poi* was twirled and beaten back with the left hand. Twirling all the time, the *poi* was bounced over the shoulder and to the flanks, thighs, knees and head, in perfect time to the songs sung by the leaders. Some dancers were able to perform with two *poi* or even four.

Oratory and song were associated forms of expression, linked through common imagery and, though less directly, through *tau marae*, songs introduced into formal speeches at the assembly. Both oratory and song derived much of their substance from mythology; both claimed poetic licence in distorting grammar in the cause of harmony; both possessed special significance for each particular *hapu* and tribe.

Spoken prose other than formal *marae* orations was poetic and full of allusions to tribal history back to the ancestral canoes (and to Hawaiki beyond the sea), to mythology, and to the attributes of birds, fish, trees and the forces of nature. Famous myths and sagas were repeated from generation to generation in a customary form with striking imagery, dramatic dialogue and appropriate songs. There was much play on words and, in more homely gatherings, riddles, jokes and particularly proverbs were told, which even spread from tribe to tribe.

The chief orator on an important occasion, such as a welcome to

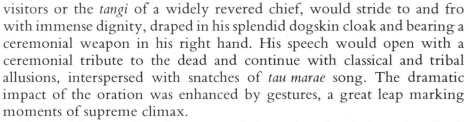

visitors or the *tangi* of a widely revered chief, would stride to and fro with immense dignity, draped in his splendid dogskin cloak and bearing a ceremonial weapon in his right hand. His speech would open with a ceremonial tribute to the dead and continue with classical and tribal allusions, interspersed with snatches of *tau marae* song. The dramatic impact of the oration was enhanced by gestures, a great leap marking moments of supreme climax.

The significance of *karakia*, or sacred chants, has already been described. They were the property of *tohunga*, priests or specially learned men, in each tribe or *hapu*. Sacred chants and spells were characterized by the intensely emotive associations postulated between all manner of material objects – mountains, birds clouds, stones – and the spiritual forces that controlled the world of men; the objects acquired *mauri* or spiritual essence in the course of the ceremonies of which *karakia* were a part. Here, for instance, is a *karakia* that accompanied the cooking and eating of a sacred meal to accomplish the lifting of a *tapu*, as on the completion of a canoe:

Light, light the holy fire
O Tiki, it burns on the sacred morning
Give us, O give us, O Tiki,
The sweetness of food; it burns
Burns for thee, the juice of the pigeon,
Burns for thee, juice of the owl,
Burns for thee, juice of the parrot,
Burns for thee, juice of the fantail,
For thee, the sweetness of the eel
From what source?
From the spring where the sky turns red –
Let it be poured.

(from Mitcalfe, *Maori Poetry*)

Waiata, or songs, were of many kinds – there were chants of lonely sentinels whiling away the long hours on the ramparts of a *pa*, humorous songs, lullabies, and so on. But most of the ones that have survived (apart from *karakia*) are *waiata tangi*, songs of mourning, and *waiata aroha*, love songs

A tune was started with an intoning note to give the correct pitch. The song would then continue on the same note, varied upwards and downwards over only three or four notes at intervals of quarter tones or less. Tempo was constant but rhythm was complex. Songs of mourning and sad love songs (most were sad) were divided into long phrases ending in the drawn out sound 'e-e-i', on a falling pitch. Singers covered each other's breaks for breathing since any break in the melody boded ill. This was a reminder that any song was the property of the *hapu* and of the ancestors. Songs linked mythology and present-day reality, dealt with the interwoven worlds of the symbolic essence of things and the destiny of mankind, and so themselves shared elements of *tapu* and *mana*.

The Maori were light-hearted as well, and their humour was earthy. Here is a satirical canoe song composed in 1840 by a Maori boat's crew to tease a *pakeha* (European) named Cook who was pressing his suit, not too successfully, with a lady named Kora from Hauraki.

Ah Kora, who gave her that beautiful gown? Teena!
Ee hoa Cookie, why do you frown? Kumea!
A Pakeha came to our pa one night. Teena!
And next day appears Kora in clothes so bright. Kumea!

Previous pages left and right: Putorino, or flute trumpet, made in the eighteenth or early nineteenth century. This instrument can be played as a flute, by blowing across the top, or as a trumpet. The putorino has one note which is modified by closing the centre hole, whichever way it is played. It was used to signal a chief's return, and also for playing waiata (sung poems).

Above: Nguru, open-tube flutes made in wood. The nguru has several holes and is blown sideways across the wide end. It has often been said that words were spoken into these flutes, but actually, this was an illusion: the tunes of certain waiata evoked the familiar words so strongly that they seemed even to be part of the music. The larger nguru has unfinished decoration in the Hokianga style of Northland. The smaller one, which is less than eight centimetres long, is decorated in the style of Wanganui.

Ah Kora, she wants a panama hat. Teena!
Te Cookie will surely give his love that. Kumea!
How pretty she'll look in her new pootae. Teena!
With love in her heart, and thanks in her eye. Huu-a-a!

(from Mead, *Traditional Maori Clothing*)

Waiata aroha were nearly always composed by women. This was natural considering that women initiated nearly all love affairs in old-time Maori society. Many of these songs are poignant and of very great beauty.

The song that follows is an exception in that it was composed by a man who fell in love with his friend's wife, Wai. The Pleiades, whose appearance marked the Maori new year, symbolized fruitfulness. Manahuna was believed by the Ngati Kahungunu to be the ancestral guardian of fish. Haumia was the god of the fern root.

There Pleiades rises slowly from the sea –
You come like a sign from the one I love
From whom I had to turn.
I am a vessel beating into the wind,
A wind that always blows ill,
I cannot tack, I am borne
Into the distance
I will go to the fish of the sea, my friend,
To the offspring of Manahuna, the last born
Of Tane, birds for the long winter's night,
And the gift of Haumia, fern root
For the long days of hunger.
Let it be so, O Wai, we must be long apart
Lest we be one together,
I honour you but fear my own weakness;
You blush, yet turn away
From the sound of my heart.
For your small heaps of food, my friend,
I have a hundred kits to give the crowd,
My name forces its way out,
Though I stand here in my place.

(from Mitcalfe, *Maori Poetry*)

Rangiira was an ageing woman, whose lover had forsaken her for a younger. Her song opens:

Rise, oh oncoming wave,
And break in two at the river mouth.
Oh tears, gush down!
During the stillness of the night
There come stealing from the heart
Reminiscences of my youth.

(from Mead, 'Imagery . . . in Maori Chants')

In the rest of the chant the composer builds up image after image revealing why she likened herself to a wave broken in two and (later) to a canoe overturned and abandoned on the beach. Many images in love

songs composed by women were connected with canoes. The canoe responds to the paddler as she to her lover's caresses.

Mountains, commonly symbols of tribal identity, took on a special significance in women's love songs. Such mountains as the lofty (male) Tongariro was the legendary lover of the graceful bush-clad Pihanga. Thus a wind blowing from a mountain meant a wind of love and to be taken to the top of a mountain peak was a synonym for orgasm, as in the following lines from a Whanganui *waiata aroha*:

I saw Tukaiora clearly,
As she lay unclad with you, oh Kaihinu,
No one to take me now to the top of (Mount) Takinikini.

(from Mead, 'Imagery . . . in Maori Chants')

Waiata tangi, or laments for the dead, were very often composed by women, though women's role in the *tangihanga* ceremonies was not confined to composing and singing the mourning songs. At the death of a close relative they were expected to tear their hair, gash their faces with stone or toothed knives and exhibit an absolute frenzy of grief.

As an example of a woman's lament, here are the first lines of Hera Hawai's grieving for her dead son:

The pain within gnaws on;
Hasten, so that I may soon die
Lest I remain longer, wandering listlessly,
Weak from hunger, faint as with summer heat.

(from Mead, 'Imagery . . . in Maori Chants')

Women's compositions tend to be more personal in their expression of anguish, whereas the men's songs dwell more on the warlike attributes of the deceased. But this distinction does not always hold good. The *tangi* which follows was composed about 1700 by Makere of the Ati-Awa for his grandchild Taramoana, who, when out gathering vines on the borderland between their territories, was ambushed, slain, and then eaten by the Ngati Ruanui.

O my son,
Only your name remains;
Now you are gone, alone.
Love has no power to restore the heart,
So slow to live, so swift to die.

Your bones lie like a necklace
At the throat of the sky,
Your blood soaks into the wood,
But you have flown –
You will greet your ancestors,
The great await thee,
Will spread soft mats
Sprinkle strange scents
And young girls will dance.
Go my son,
And may this poor song
Go with thee;
Words tell only of my inadequacy.

* * * *

I will go to the ridge of Okawa
I will pluck out his liver
That will show these men
What I mean when I speak of revenge.

Where is the man that could kill you?
Where is the hand that defiled you?
No! The gods
Willed you to die,
Tore out your heart and lungs,
Splintered bones and spattered brains
Like vomit, ribs picked clean
And blood oozing through the stones
Of the feast.
Let your foul cousins taste
The sweetness of their ancestress
In thy breast. Mairie-i-rangi
Will lie like a stone in their belly.

* * * *

You dart like a shag beneath
the dark waters of the stream,
Dive like a gannet to a death
In the deep where small fish gleam.
O my great fish, rise from the depths.
No! That cannot be,
Death has swallowed thee.

(from Mitcalfe, *Maori Poetry*)

102

Without doubt; special horror was added to the incident in Maori eyes because Taramoana was a kinsman of some of the Ngati Ruanui, and to eat his body transgressed the most sacred bonds of kinship, being equivalent to eating their common ancestress. After this incident, the law of *utu*, blood revenge, overrode all ties between them, and they remained ever after implacable enemies.

These lines contrast sharply with the following tribute to a powerful chief composed by a man:

Farewell oh mighty one; farewell oh feared one;
Farewell, oh sheltering rata (tree) from the north wind,
The tribes, alas, are disconsolate and bowed down.

(from Buck, *The Coming of the Maori*)

Mount Egmont from Lake Wangamahoe. Above: Egmont on a rare day when he is not covered in cloud. Left: Egmont hidden by clouds. The Maori personified many forms of nature, and the speech of the Rangatira was full of mythopoetic allusions expressing anthropomorphic ideas. There are many myths with different variations concerning volcanic mountains, which are both male and female, and have very definite personalities. Here are two which explain why Mount Egmont (originally Taranaki) is almost always hidden in cloud. Egmont, a dormant male volcano, lived near the female volcano Ruapehu in the land of the vulcans, the Hauhungaroa range to the east. Egmont and Ruapehu fell in love and eloped, fleeing to the west. But when Ruapehu became tired, Egmont did not want to stop, and went on until the sea halted him. By then, he could not go back, and realizing that he had lost Ruapehu forever, he hid his face, and has been weeping ever since. Another version has it that one day when Egmont was out hunting, his beloved Ruapehu was courted and won by another mountain, Tongariro. Egmont came back and surprised them. A terrific battle ensued, in which Tongariro and Egmont hurled fire, lava and rocks at each other. Egmont was defeated, and retreated to the West Coast, carving the channel of the Wanganui River as he went. He was guided to his final resting place by a rock, Te Toka-a-Rauhotu, which then remained near Cape Egmont. Two smaller female mountains settled next to him, in love with him and faithful, but Egmont stands towering above them and gazing towards Ruapehu and his rival. In spite of her affair with Tongariro, Ruapehu still loves Egmont, and the cloud which drifts eastward from his head is a sign of his love for her.

TU MATAUENGA
The God of War

Intertribal warfare was endemic in New Zealand and virtually an integral component of the Maori kinship system. Given the Maori's preoccupation with prestige, any insult or injury was viewed as sufficient cause for more or less violent retribution. Feuds and fighting maintained the *mana* of the *hapu* and of individual chiefs and warriors. Even as tradition, the peaceful world of the Moa Hunters was forgotten. As population pressures increased and tribes came into conflict, every adult male became a warrior and scattered dwellings gave way to fortified strongholds, or *pa tuwatawata*.

To paraphrase Phelps' excellent summary: If a woman married outside her tribe any mistreatment by her husband was considered an insult to her whole tribe; disrespectful references, *tapu* infringements or killings were also transgressions requiring the implementation of the principle of payment, *utu*, or blood vengence. The execution of this principle normally took the form of a military raid (*taua muru*), and, even if the original culprit escaped personal retribution, his *hapu* was held responsible and was obliged to pay. This raid was then considered a violation by those attacked. who would in turn exact *utu* to restore their damaged *mana*. This system inevitably led to continuous warfare in the form of reciprocal reprisal raiding, ambushes, treachery and assaults on enemy *pa*. Pitched battles were uncommon, for the maximum honour was obtained by destroying the most enemies preferably by cunning and economical means – like slaughtering the guests at a peace conference.

Land conquests were infrequent unless an enemy became permanently decimated. Though wars were fought on points of honour (at least overtly) rather than for reasons of direct material gain, booty in the form of greenstone and other precious objects was welcomed; more so the bodies of the slain. Men, women and children were slaughtered and eaten, except for any that could claim kinship and the handful who were enslaved. Maori fighting was essentially hand to hand with stabbing spears and a variety of long and short thrusting and slashing clubs. The use of projectile weapons like thrown spears or rocks was almost entirely confined to the defenders of *pas*, and slings and bows and arrows were unknown.

The three kinds of Maori long-club were the *pouwhenua*, the *tewhatewha* and the *taiaha*. All were about 1.5 metres (5 feet) long and were made from a single piece of tough wood. All had a striking blade at one end and a stabbing point at the other. They were thus dual purpose club-spears. The use of these weapons was as much an art as European swordsmanship.

Short clubs, whose generic name was *patu*, were also of three types,

Preserved head of a Maori warrior who was killed by a blow to the back of his head. The tattoo is unique, in that on the cheeks are figures resembling tikis.

mere (more properly referring to a greenstone *patu*), *kotiate*, a symmetrical weapon with deep side notches, and *wahaika*, its asymmetrical counterpart. The spatulate ends of all three types were ground to a sharp edge which extended down the sides. A strip of dogskin was put through a hole in the handle and tied in a loop for passing over the thumb and around the hand. *Patu* were used for quick in-fighting in which a fraction of a second was too important to waste in raising the weapon to strike a downward blow. Thus, the technique was a thrust or a half-arm jab with the sharp front end of the club to the temple, neck or ribs and as the enemy was falling, the butt or heel delivered a downward blow to the skull. The dogskin loop prevented the hand from slipping and the force of the thrust being weakened. The Maori short clubs (and their early eastern-Polynesian counterparts) were not only unique in form but also in being designed for a forward thrust instead of the downward blow characteristic of other forms of clubs.

From early boyhood, the guards, strokes, feints and parries with the various weapons, long and short, were carefully learned and assiduously practised. The accompanying footwork consisted of short, quick jumps with both feet off the ground, the right and left being alternately advanced in landing. In this way, opponents sparred round each other seeking an opening. With long clubs the blows were quick and short so that the club could be brought back quickly to guard the body. A full swing which, on missing, carried the weapon too far for quick recovery was condemned. Buck describes the 'withering contempt' of an old Maori watching the overswinging of clubs at an arms drill display, who muttered '*He kai na te ahi*', meaning that in the old days the careless ones would have become food for their opponents.

In advancing to single combat the long club was held vertically in front of the mid-line of the body with the blade above and the point below and the right hand gripping the shaft above the left. The club was inclined to the right or left with the sparring movements of the body and was in position to parry with the least movement any blows aimed at the head or any thrusts aimed at the body. A blow from above with the blade was termed *whitipu*; a thrust from below with the point was called *whakarehu*. The *whakarehu* thrust was usually a feint to draw the opponent's guard and so clear the way for a quick *whitipu* blow at the head. However, if the thrust went home, well and good.

A warrior usually carried a *patu* thrust through his belt in addition to his long club. Some warriors preferred the short clubs. They were dangerous in-fighters who depended on agility to evade the blows from the long clubs.

In combat, it was advisable to watch, not the eyes, but the big toes of an opponent. Feint blows were made from the flexed elbows, and the feet did not need to take a firm stance at the moment of delivery. A real blow came from the shoulders of the opponent, and, in taking a firm stance, he gripped the ground with his toes. An alternative to watching for the flexing of the big toe of the advanced foot was to watch the shoulder for the ripple of the deltoid muscle that heralded a real blow.

In addition to weapons training, men were taught ritual chants to strengthen them spiritually. For instance:

> *Give me my belt,*
> *Give me my loin cloth,*

On Banks Peninsula, Akaroa Harbour with Onawe Peninsula.

The peak of the pa on Onawe Peninsula, with fortification remains. Onawe pa is the first example of a trench defence designed to be defended with muskets. In 1828, Te Rauparaha of the northern Ngati Toa tribe attacked another pa just north of Christchurch, inventing a zigzag trench to allow his musket-armed warriors to approach the palisade, which was defended by half a dozen muskets. He took the pa, vowing to return. During the next two years the Ngai Tahu developed Onawe to be defended by muskets. The outer ditch was made shallow so that a man with a gun could kneel in it and fire out under a palisade. The bank behind the ditch was given a flat top and the inside slope angled for the same reason. At each corner and at intervals along the sides, crossfire angles were placed to cover the front of the outer palisade. Onawe pa appeared so strong that Te Rauparaha decided not to attack it, but tricked the defendants into allowing him and his men inside to talk peace, and then destroyed them. This pa is really the beginning of trench warfare, which was to see its full development in the 1845 war between the Maori and the Europeans in the Northland area. The ideas were taken back to England by British Army units.

That they may be put on,
That they may be fastened
That wrath and I may join together,
Rage and I.
The loin cloth is for anger;
The loin cloth is for destroying war parties.

(from Buck, *The Coming of the Maori*)

The Maori *pa* or fortified settlement was invariably sited to make the best use of the natural defensive features of the ground. Depending on local conditions, the main earthworks might be scarped terraces, trenches or ramparts, but each line of defence was surmounted by a stockade and sometimes overtopped by fighting platforms. Each line of fortifications had a narrow gateway protected by a blind of palisading to lay enemies open to flank attack. Houses and food storage buildings were within the defence lines, while on the highest ground behind the innermost fortifications was the stronghold's citadel, which was both the ultimate rallying point and the site of the houses of the principal chief and his relatives.

Vayda, who has written the most authoritative work on Maori warfare, notes that sometimes part of the population resided outside the *pa* and only retired inside on threat of attack. There were also seasonal fishing, fowling and cultivation camps which, however, were often protected with light stockades, there being several transitional forms between the heavily fortified *pa* and the open *kainga* village.

Such spectacular scarped terraces as those ringing Auckland's extinct volcanoes tend to give a false impression of regional uniformity in Maori defensive works. In fact, *pa* were only common in Iwitini, the northern and coastal region of the North Island, and even there they varied considerably. The forts of Taranaki, Bay of Plenty and Waikato were smaller than those of Auckland and the Bay of Islands and relied on ramparts and trenches rather than terraced escarpments. Even less elaborate were the forts of the Ngati Porou of Poverty Bay, for they put more faith in their wild coast and rugged hinterland. The same applied in inland Waenganui, where *pa* were few and simple. There was a tendency to seek protection in natural fastnesses such as forests or impregnable cliffs. A Tuhoe tribesman said to Best: 'The rugged canyons were our stockades; the steep ranges and dense forests were our earthworks.'

While there was thus no such thing as a typical *pa*, Cook's and Banks's account of a fort they visited in 1769 at Mercury Bay has the virtue of describing an indubitably pre-European construction. It was built on a high promontory 'in some places quite inaccessible to man', and elsewhere 'defended by a double ditch, a bank and 2 rows of Picketing, the inner row upon the Bank'. There was ample room for men to walk and handle their arms between the picketing and the inner ditch. The outer stockade was slanted inwards. The depth of the inner ditch was 7.3 metres (24 feet). Inside the stockade was a platform 9 metres (29.5 feet) high and 12 metres long; a number of darts lay upon it to throw down upon assailants. Another, similar stage flanked the first.

Beside the works on the land side just described, the 'whole Village was Pallisaded round with a line of pretty strong Picketing run round the Edge of the hill'. The ground within had been levelled into the form of little amphitheatres, 'each of them Pallisaded round, and had communication one with another by narrow lanes and little gateways, which could easily be stopped up, so that if an Enemy had forced the outer Picketing he had several others to encounter'. The number of internal palisaded enclosures was twenty, each with between one and fourteen houses. Gourds and kumara (sweet potatoes) were planted inside the *pa* but the nearest permanent water was a brook under the hill. Cook noted that an 'immense quantity of Fern root and a good many dry'd fish' had been layed in and supposed that water was stored in gourds. He summed up his impressions: 'Upon the whole I looked upon it to be a very strong and and well chose Post, and where a small number of resolute men might defend themselves a long time against a vast superior force.'

The conduct of military campaigns was in part conditioned by efforts to defend or take (preferably by surprise) such fortified strongholds as the formidable fortress at Mercury Bay, but there were many other aspects of Maori strategy. Food supplies were never very abundant in old New Zealand, so major operations were largely restricted to the summer and autumn months when good fern root, berries, fish and kumara would be available. Since transport was by foot along forest tracks or beaches, or else by canoe, war parties must largely live off the country and were well advised to carry no more than a parrot carried in its claw. The restriction on *tapu* warriors carrying food was obviated by their bearing what little bundles of fern-root paste they needed in their *noa* (left) hands.

The *hapu* was the strongest Maori political-kinship unit and so was most often engaged on 'the red trail of Tu'. *Hapu* varied enormously in size. One could generally muster from 100 to 300 fighting men for a campaign. Several *hapu* or a whole tribe might combine in war, but for one side to field a thousand men at once in pre-musket days must have been very unusual. Indeed, because of transport and commissariat limitations some chiefs preferred to lead war parties of as few as fifty specially chosen warriors. War leaders took part in battles with their men, just as high chiefs cultivated their plantations with their own hands. The *mana* of an *ariki* was such that he usually led in war as in peace. Sometimes, however, due to age or lack of inclination, the titular high chief was unsuited

A kotiate, a bilobed wooden stabbing club probably from the Gisborne area of the North Island. Maori warriors fought hand to hand, using short clubs, patu, like this one, for thrusting and parrying. Patu, meaning 'to strike' is the word for all short clubs.

The Mangapiko River Valley, site of the 'battle of the muskets'. On this spot stood a pa. In 1822, some 5000 Waikato warriors armed only with traditional weapons were attacked by 3000 Ngapuhi carrying muskets. Some 3000 perished, mostly defenders.

for a military role and another high-born member of the senior *rangatira* line held the position of war chief.

The basically forested character of New Zealand and the narrowness of the foot tracks that wound across country, dictated single file as the usual order of march, with its implications of strung-out columns and the consequent possibilities for ambush. Hence the importance of scouts and especially of the most alert and bravest of them all, the two advance scouts, termed *kiore,* or 'bush rats'. Tuta Nihoniho, an officer with the Ngati Porou Native Contingent in the 1860s, recorded the advice he had learned from the old men of his tribe. This was to march in open order, and not in the foolish manner of the Europeans, and to have scouts out front and rear.

And let the scouts in front have two *kiore* out ahead of them to search the forests, and gullies, and rocks for your enemies. Because these *kiore* are persons who have been handed over to death they were separated, so that if one of them be captured the other escapes to convey the news to the scouts behind and to the main body.

Any wayfarer crossing the line of a war party was immediately killed. Though this may have been partly for reasons of security, it seems more likely that it was to maintain the sanctity of the war *tapu*.

Maori battles, whether open fight or ambuscade, were usually brief. The loss of a war chief or champion (*toa*) would so dishearten a contingent (not because they lost their courage, but because the gods had withdrawn their favour) that they would at once break off the engagement and often flee in disorder – at which time they were most readily cut down by their pursuers. A single major encounter might terminate a campaign, but a strong enough war party might remain in enemy territory for months, ravaging the cultivations and food storehouses and materially supplementing their diet with the corpses of the slain.

All the evidence points to the extreme rarity of pitched battles in the days before firearms altered the character of Maori warfare (and led to the extermination of whole sub-tribes). When mass encounters did take place they were probably largely accidental, as revealed by the following account, written by a Maori.

. . . a Nga Puhi war party came to attack Te Kerekere, a Ngati Awa fort on the other side of the valley from the main Kaitaia settlement of today. The Nga Puhi pitched camp at Oinu and at night sent two scouts to reconnoitre the enemy *pa*. Entering the *pa*, the scouts were able to move about and gain information. Finally they were apprehended and one was killed. The other escaped and reported back to his camp. Some Nga Puhi regarded the killing of one of the scouts as an ill omen and advised a return home. The Nga Puhi leader then rose and said: 'Let the cowards return and the warriors follow me.' All the Nga Puhi remained. During the night they proceeded towards the enemy *pa* with the intention of taking it by surprise. Meanwhile, Te Whiti, the Ngati Awa chief, had addressed his people in the following strain: 'The army of Nga Puhi has arrived. Be brave! Be courageous! We will go to meet the enemy. Be brave!' During the night Te Whiti and his warriors sallied forth to surprise Nga Puhi. Thus, the two parties, both intent on surprise, happened to meet on the plain and they did their fighting there.

(from A. P. Vayda, *Maori Warfare*)

As in other cultures, the apparent cause of a war in Maori society was not necessarily the real, underlying cause. Thus, in wars that were fought over infringements of *tapu*, *maakutu* (witchcraft) or for *utu*, what was often really being decided was the right to possession of food supplies or of particularly desirable fishing or fowling resources. Not that permanent occupation of conquered land was common, but it did occur, and over the centuries must have significantly contributed to the distribution of population.

Of course, in many cases the overt and actual causes of hostilities were the same. The principle that an injury or insult to one was equally a slight to all his or her kindred, and demanded *utu* before the account could be squared, ensured that there were always plenty of *take mui* (grievances demanding redress in blood). Full-scale warfare was not necessarily the result. The institution of the *taua muru,* or plundering expedition (described earlier), was sometimes a very effective means of cooling passions and gaining satisfaction, though resentments aroused could sow the seeds of future conflicts. *Utu* could also be obtained by witchcraft or by degrading the offenders' dead by fashioning implements from their bones.

But active warfare was never far away from the Classic Maori. As Vayda points out, the need to have a *take*, or pretext for hostilities, did little to mitigate the likelihood of surprise raids because *take* were always to hand. Fresh trouble might arise over rights to land or fishing grounds, but there were generally adjustments to be made for injuries committed perhaps generations ago. The memory of unavenged injuries was handed down as an heirloom, and the obligation of *utu* was a first lesson for Maori children. E. Shortland, a scholar and Protector of Aborigines in New Zealand in the 1850s, stated that account was kept of the warlike exploits and offences that the group (whether *hapu* or tribe) made against others and that others made against the group. His Maori informants gave him a debtor and creditor account of offences extending over eight generations.

A maripi tuatini, or shark-tooth knife. These were not used for ordinary jobs, but for that most tapu of tasks, cutting up human flesh. Length 21.8 cm.

Since, as a rule, one group or the other would regard itself as in arrears, the prospect of hostilities was ever present.

There was thus a need for unremitting vigilance to guard against surprise. During Cook's visit in 1769 Banks described how the Maori in a fishing camp disposed themselves for the night:

> Women and children were plac'd innermost or farthest from the Sea, the Men lay in a kind of half Circle round them, and on the Trees close by them were ranged their arms in order so no doubt they are afraid of an attack from some Enemy not far off.

There was a great deal of justice in the old Maori saying, 'Birds sleep sound and peaceful upon a tree branch, but man, he is ever wakeful and in dread of enemies.'

Surprise attacks, including the most treacherous ones, were the order of the day in old New Zealand. Guests (and hosts) at intertribal gatherings were always at risk, whether the occasion was peace-making, a wedding or a *tangi* for a dead chief. All went prudently armed, but this was not always enough. When an important Ngati Whatua chief died about the middle of the eighteenth century, tribes in any way connected with the deceased were invited to the feast of mourning. Among those accepting was *ariki* Kiwi from the Auckland isthmus. At a signal his followers turned on their Ngati Whatua hosts and slaughtered them. Another story concerns the widely feared Te Rauparaha. When he was raiding the Wairarapa in the 1820s he invited the defenders to a feast where peace would be made. Some 350 guests arrived and were seated alternatively with their hosts. When the guests began to eat, Te Rauparaha gave a signal for concealed weapons to be drawn and the guests were cut down to a man.

More orthodox stratagems (in Western eyes) were the various forms of surprise attack that were practised – ambush, use of rain storms as concealing covers in rushing a *pa*, mock retreat followed by ambushed counter-attack, disguise as simple farmers or fishers. When battle was joined, particularly formal engagements, great significance was attached to the killing of the first of the enemy, *mata ika*, the 'first fish'. The *whangai hau* ritual, in which the *tohunga* cut out the victim's heart and offered it to the tribal war god, was performed on the battlefield. The ambition to slay the first fish, says Buck, often led warriors to take undue risks and so provide a first fish for the enemy. Thus the warrior Te Rangihiroa (after whom Buck himself was named) sprang off a high embankment into a fully armed war canoe in his search for fame. His action is thus described in a lament for his death.

Swift as a bird
To catch the first fish
Lest the name decline.

(from Buck, *The Coming of the Maori*)

Single combat was an established institution, especially when two opposing forces were drawn up in battle array and had worked themselves up in the frenzy of the war *haka*. A noted warrior would rush forward to challenge an equally notable opponent. If the duel resulted in the slaying of the leader of one party his followers often abandoned the field on the spot. Otherwise general battle would be joined. Though one or two seconds were sometimes provided for each contestant, Maori single-handed encounters lacked the strict formality of European duels. The

The post named Uenuku, archaic symbol of Uenukuwhatu, a tribal god of the Waikato people and personification of the rainbow (the prongs represent a rainbow). According to tradition Uenuku was first carried to the Kawhia Harbour on the ancestral Tainui canoe from 'Hawaiki' in a small sculpture. When the canoe landed, he was given this larger sculpture as his resting place. (When aid was needed away from home, he was asked to inhabit a small sculpture, which was carried by the war party, or ambassadors.) Uenuku stayed in the care of the family of the original finder of the relic, but was buried during a feud in a swamp, and lost for generations. It was found by chance in 1906 by a non-Maori, and lent to the Wanganui Museum. There it was rediscovered by a Maori woman, member of the guardian family, and it is now again in the possession of the family, which had searched for it for years (though in fact it is kept in a museum).

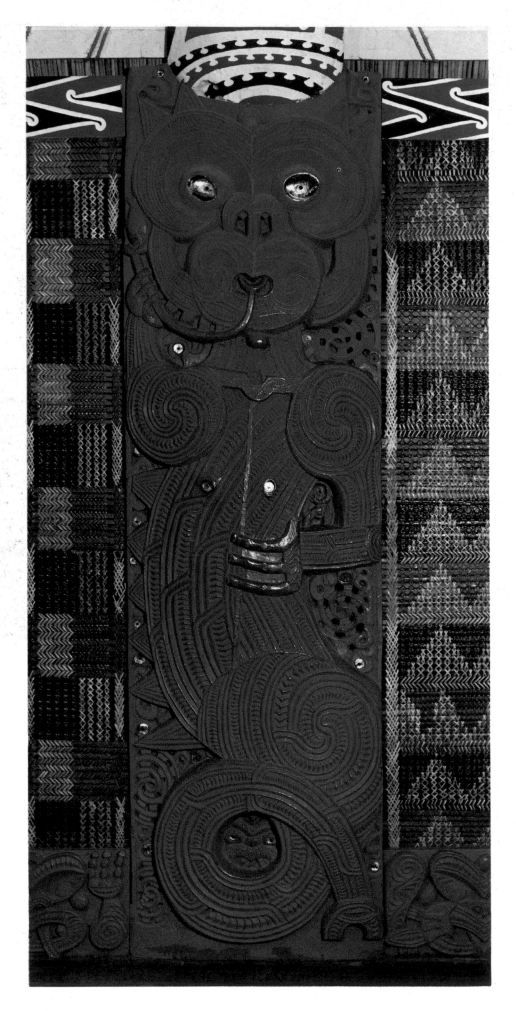

Ancestral panel in Hotunui, a meeting house carved as a wedding gift by Ngati Awa of Whakatane for the Ngati Maru of Thames. This panel has the form of a marakihau named Ureia, a guardian sea monster of the Thames people. He was invited to visit the Manukau Harbour at Auckland by the taniwha there called Haumia, who told him in good faith that the people living around the harbour were kind. Ureia came and found they had made a special house for him in the sea, but in reality it was a trap in which he was killed. His disillusioned friend Haumia left the harbour never to return. The death of Ureia was one of the causes of the Ngati Maru attack on the Auckland area in 1700.

seconds might, on occasion, intervene and so might others. Thus Poriro, a member of a besieged garrison, sallied forth to single combat with Mou, chief of the attacking force. Mou caught his antagonist by his long hair and proceeded to drag him away. But a sister of Poriro attacked Mou and struck him down with a stone. Each protagonist chose his own weapons and any device was permitted. One warrior most effectively opened the proceedings by scooping up a handful of sand and throwing it in his opponent's eyes.

Captives in battle were rarely spared. Apart from becoming one of the relatively few slaves that could be accommodated in the Maori economy, the only salvation was to claim kinship with the victors. Generally, in the words of an old Arawa chief, 'Ka mate, ka hainga, ka kai!' – 'They died, they were cooked, they were eaten!' This fate applied equally to combatants and non-combatants, men, women and children. Mortality in tribal wars would have been even higher had not the New Zealand rain-forest abounded in secret and remote hiding-places. The Maori attitude to killing opponents was well expressed by Toenga Pou of the Nga Puhi:

You ask . . . if it is not better to save the life of an enemy, when you

Karaka Point, Queen Charlotte Sound, sacred burial ground and site of an ancient pa. Queen Charlotte Sound is the natural gateway to the South Island. When the Rangitane moved across Cook Strait from the Horowhenua following Captain Cook's visits, they settled at Karaka Point, whence they were expelled by the Ngai Tahu. The Rangitane then settled in the Wairau River mouth area in Cloudy Bay to the south, where they still are.

117

Right: Te Oha, a storehouse erected c.1820 by Ngati Whakaue, chief Haere Huka, at Mourca. Storehouses of this type were symbols of community mana.

Below: A fishhook of human bone with double inner barb. This type was developed on the East Coast of the North Island, but this particular hook comes from Banks Peninsula. The Ngai Tahu tribe, who are still dominant in the South Island, migrated from the Gisborne area of the North Island in the seventeenth and eighteenth centuries; they took cannibalism with them into the South Island. To make a fishhook of an enemy warrior's bone would have been an especially marked insult, and a provocation which would force the opposing tribe to battle, even if it had been inclined towards peace.

Burnt forest in the Tasman Mountains, at the extreme north of the South Island.

have rendered him helpless, than to kill him? No, it is not better; neither is it wise. What is the use of getting a man down, if you are fighting with him during war time, or wounding him, unless you finish your work by killing him? Never, even, let him get up again; that would be . . . a future source of trouble . . . For your enemy will not cease to remember that you once got him down (but refrained from killing him because he was not worth it) until he has either killed you; or someone else, even if only remotely your relative . . . If ever you go to fight, fight for results; if not, stay at home and do not make a fool of yourself.

Maori cannibalism went hand-in-glove with warfare and was rarely practised otherwise. The stigma of having an ancestor eaten lasted for many generations. Buck describes a contemporary incident where one old man taunted another with the words, 'The flesh of your ancestor is still sticking between my teeth,' opening his mouth and pointing to his teeth to make his point clearer. His companion promptly knocked him down, knelt on his chest, and was opening his pocket-knife to cut his throat when bystanders intervened.

The story of Ngatokorua, told by Buck, shows how a brave man saved his descendents from the stigma of his having been eaten. He was wounded in battle but managed to break off the point of his spear and conceal it in his clenched right hand before he was finally overpowered. He was tied with his arms behind his back and left lying on the ground. He managed to free his hands but kept them behind his back as if still bound. He then called the high chief of the enemy who came over to him. Ngatokorua raised his face to indicate that he wished to press noses in farewell. As the chief bent down, Ngatokorua seized him by the hair with his left hand, pulled him down, and stabbed him in the neck with the spear point held in his right hand. The blood gushed down and Ngatokorua managed to daub it over his face and body before the startled warriors killed him. Ngatokorua died happy. His body had been rendered *tapu* to the war party by the blood of their chief and they could not eat him.

As great a disgrace as being eaten was to be made a slave. While slaves' children were free, they and their descendants were always liable to be taunted with this blot on their escutcheon. From Buck again comes the story of how another brave man avoided this disgrace. Te Whakauruhanga, a high chief of the Ngati Maniopoto was speared through the thighs and captured during an affray with the Arawa. The wounded chief thought of his unblemished line and pondered deeply on how he could influence his captors to take his life. Then he thought of a solution. 'What leading chiefs had been killed in the engagement?' he enquired (the standing of Maori battles was measured by the prominence of the slain). 'None,' he was told. So Whakauruhanga, lifting his head with dignity and assurance, commanded, 'Kill me so that your battle may have a name.'

Maori peace-making was generally initiated by the less successful side, though a prudent war party usually withdrew from enemy territory before local allies could be gathered against it, so there was not necessarily any formal declaration of peace. Hostilities were simply suspended until such time, perhaps years hence, when it suited one of the protagonists to resume them. But embassies were sent to opponents and agreements made that were sealed by gifts. The most durable agreement was one cemented by marriage to a high chief's daughter. Women rarely took part in the actual fighting, but their role in initiating new bonds of intertribal kinship was important. Nevertheless, even at the best of times, peace was fragile.

Vayda tells the story of a woman's successful peace embassy. Te Heuheu, the Taupo chief, told his daughter, Te Rohu, to go as an envoy of peace to a strong Ngati Kahungunu war party that was approaching. 'Would you give me up to be killed?' the daughter objected. Te Heuheu answered, 'Not so, for your mother is closely related to them.' So Te Rohu went, together with six of the Taupo men, each with a flax circlet emblem of peace tied round his head. On this occasion, peace was successfully concluded, but it is very unlikely that the embassy would have been respected were it not for Te Rohu's kinship with the attackers.

Were there any positive features of this terrible institution of warfare? Here, in essence, is Vayda's view, which seems an eminently fair one.

Regular forms of public justice in the relations between Maori communities were virtually confined to the *taua muru* (limited plundering raid). There were no inter-community mechanisms of authority, other than shaky alliances. In the absence of such mechanisms, war was useful as a redress for serious intertribal offences and as a deterrent against further such offences. The kind of offences for which a group sooner or later took retaliatory action included insults, poaching on food preserves, homicide, violence or magical aggression.

It was obviously desirable to have protection against trespassers on preserves of birds, fish, rats, berries, or fern root. The protection of members of the group from loss or injury inflicted by outsiders helped keep it together and maintain the numbers and morale necessary for co-operation in the tasks of subsistence and defence.

An anecdote by Buck also suggests that the old-time warrior values had more than a little virtue and that they remain a positive force for the future. A young boy, a contemporary of Buck, was brought up by his granduncle, who still thought young chiefs should be trained as warriors. When the old man had to go outside at night to relieve himself, he slapped the sleeping child, and went back to bed muttering words of disappointment. This went on for some time, until, on one memorable occasion, the child, by this time apprehensive, awoke to hear the old man leave the room. When he returned to slap the sleeper, the child gazed up at him. A pleased look came into the old man's eyes and he went to bed, saying, 'Now I have a grandchild who will be a bulwark of defence to his tribe.' After that they played a game. Some mornings the old man got up earlier, others later, but always the child gazed up at him, wide awake. The training had had its effect – the child roused to the slightest sound.

Another time, the child fell on his face and lay crying. Instead of being fussed over, a stick descended sharply on his upturned backside. He turned over and saw his granduncle raising his stick for another blow. He rolled out of reach, got to his feet and ran away. Another game was inaugurated. The boy would see how close he could fall to the old man and yet roll away before the stick could fall.

By these means the old man taught his grandnephew the elements of becoming a warrior: to wake at the slightest sound; not to remain on the ground after a fall; to evade a falling blow; and to regain his feet in the shortest possible time.

The boy was Paraire Tomoana of Hastings. Tribal warfare was long over by his day but, in spite of being born with a club foot, he became the best rugby half-back Te Aute College ever produced and he represented Hawkes Bay in rugby, cricket, hockey and tennis.

Below: War-canoe bailer in East Coast style. War canoes up to eighty feet long were made with a dugout hull with end pieces topped with sidestrakes. Despite caulking of holes and a covering batten, the joins leaked. Men with bailers shaped to fit the bottom of the hull sent out a cascade of water from wells made in the platform for the paddlers' feet. The canoe would not sink when swamped, but would lie awash.

Bottom: A war-canoe anchor stone, punga, from Tatapouri, Poverty Bay. The designs on the end are ownership marks and indicate that the anchor is for a particular war canoe. Length 40 cm.

*Until 1885, Europeans were forbidden by law to enter the King Country. When
Maori chiefs were finally forced to allow the construction of a railway line through the
King Country, they agreed only on condition that liquor would be prohibited there.
This ruling was enforced until 1955.*

EPILOGUE

It was the coming of the *pakeha* (outsiders) that abruptly ended the isolation of the 'Stone Age' Maori. The use of metal implements, the introduction of Irish potatoes and wheat, the adoption of European-style sailing craft and the spread of literacy were all very rapid. On the debit side, the flintlock musket brought unprecedented mortality to inter-tribal warfare, as northern tribes with a near-monopoly of the new weapons paid off old scores by wiping out half the population. Diseases such as measles, influenza, small pox and venereal diseases were introduced, causing devastating epidemics. In this situation the missionaries' doctrines of peace fell on ready ears. By the early 1850s, *hapu* owned and managed wheat, stock, produce farms, flour mills and coastal shipping so successfully that the Maori were feeding the growing towns of Auckland and Wellington, and more than holding their own with their European counterparts.

During the 1840s, European settlers became numerous enough to demand the taking over – by whatever means and pretexts – of the Maori land. The Land Wars of the 1860s were the final outcome. While Maori unity was never complete – some tribes remaining neutral, and others fighting on the European side – the election of a Maori King in 1859 added considerable cohesion to the central North Island tribes. Another important unifying principle was the militant Pai Marire or Hauhau region, founded by Te Ua Huamene as a synthesis of Christian and old-time beliefs.

An example of the calibre of Maori resistance is an engagement fought at Rangiriri on the Waikato River in 1863. More than a thousand British troops supported by artillery and river gunboats attacked a position held by some three hundred Maori armed with 175 firearms. Two bayonet charges by the 65th Regiment and three rifle and grenade assaults by other military and naval units were beaten off. Only when they were out of ammunition, their request for more gunpowder denied, did the survivors surrender. The following year saw the battle of the Orakau *pa* in which women took part and the young Taupo chieftainess Ahumai te Paerata made her famous reply to an offer to evacuate non-combatants: 'The women will fight alongside the men, *ake, ake, ake!*' (forever, and ever and ever!). But despite their bravery, the Maori could not stand indefinitely against the might of Victorian England, and were ultimately defeated.

Wholesale confiscation of Maori land followed. The bitter and disillusioned people turned away from white society and towards religions, sects and spiritual movements of their own. The Ringatu sect, an offshoot of Hauhauism was formed by Te Kooti Rikirangi when he was a prisoner on the Chatham Islands. After a daring escape and return to the mainland in a commandeered schooner, he carried on stubborn guerilla resistance in the Urewera and King Country, being eventually pardoned in 1883. But the most remarkably original innovation was that of the prophets Te Whiti o Rongomai and Tohu of Parihaka in Taranaki. This was a philosophy and programme of passive, non-violent resistance to the occupation of Maori land. The policy was actively pursued, despite provocation and imprisonment of the prophets and their ploughmen, all through the 1870s and 1880s. Te Whiti o Rongomai helped to revive his people's spirit and dignity; he anticipated Ghandi by sixty years.

The new century was marked by the rise of Maori parliamentary activity. Sir Apirana Ngata, for instance, was in Parliament from 1905 to 1943. Sir Maui Pomare, another graduate of Te Aute College, was instrumental in 'picking up the crumbs of the land' when a Royal Commission he helped to institute in 1926 belatedly recognized as illegal the seizure of the Waitara Block which had precipitated the Land Wars of the 1860s. Despite this moral vindication of the dispossessed Maori, the confiscated land was not returned. In the 1920s more Labour-aligned policies emerged from the political wing of the Ratana healing sect and were consolidated by electoral successes in the 1930s.

The period since World War II has been marked by a continuing radicalism. With their numbers approaching 180,000 (some scholars say many more) there are more Maori than ever before, and their birth rate considerably exceeds the European. Massive immigration of Pacific Islanders has materially added to the Polynesian population of New Zealand, and at the same time caused some new tensions. More than fifty per cent of the Maori are now city-dwellers. There are many grave problems – economic, educational and racial, but the Maori response to them continues to be dynamic. The challenge of urbanization has been met by the construction of new, traditionally decorated *marae*. In the towns these are being built at such a rate that the wood-carvers cannot meet the demand. These *marae* are becoming increasingly important centres of traditional community activities and innovative developments in all the arts. The growing Maori population is being sustained and unified by a vital and resilient *Maoritanga* (Maori culture).

Right: Swamp and bush to which 300 Maori defenders of Orakau fled, after holding off 1500 British troops.

Below: Bone pekapeka, two-headed breast ornament, Wellington area, c. 1850.

GLOSSARY

ariki high chief
atua god
haka dance
hapu clan
iwi tribe
karakia sacred chant, or invocation
kumara sweet potato
mana spiritual power or status

manaia bird man motif
marae Polynesia: temple platform. New Zealand: ceremonial ground before the tribal meeting house
mauri spiritual essence, active life principle
moko tattoo, 'skin carving'
noa ordinary – opposite of *tapu*

pa fortified hill or settlement
pakeha outsider
peruperu war dance
poi graceful woman's dance
rangatira aristocrats of chiefly descent
rei puta whale tooth pendants
tangi mourning ceremony
taniwha monster motifs

tapa bark cloth
tapu sacred
tiki human-form motifs
tohunga priest
tuahu shrines
utu blood revenge
wairua the true soul
waka canoe

BIBLIOGRAPHY

Alpers, A. *Maori Myths and Tribal Legends* Auckland 1964

Angas, G. E. *Savage Life and Scenes in Australia and New Zealand* London 1847

Angas, G. E. *New Zealanders Illustrated* London 1847; facsimile edition Wellington 1966

Banks, J. *Journal of the Right Honourable Sir Joseph Banks During Captain Cook's First Voyage* ed. J. D. Hooker, Saint Clair Shores, Missouri 1976

Barrow, T. T. *Maori Wood Sculpture* Wellington 1969

Bellwood, P. *Man's Conquest of the Pacific* Auckland 1978

Beaglehole, J. C. *The Journals of Captain Cook,* London 1969; Stanford 1972

Best, E. *Maori Myth and Religion* Wellington 1954

Best, E. *Spiritual and Mental Concepts of the Maori* (Dominion Museum Monograph no. 2) Wellington 1966

Biggs, B. *Maori Marriage* Wellington 1954

Buck, Sir P. (Te Rangi Hiroa) *The Coming of the Maori* Wellington 1966

Levison, M., R. G. Ward and J. W. Webb *The Settlement of Polynesia: a Computer Simulation* Minneapolis 1973

Lewis, D. H. *The Voyaging Stars* Sydney and London 1978

Lewis, D. H. *We the Navigators* Canberra and Honolulu 1975

McEwen, J. M. 'Maori Art' in *Encyclopedia of New Zealand* (vol. 2) Wellington 1966

Mead, S. M. 'Imagery, Symbolism and Social Values in Maori Chants' in *Journal of the Polynesian Society* (78: 3) Wellington 1969

Mead, S. M. *Traditional Maori Clothing* Honolulu 1969

Mitcalfe, B. *Maori Poetry* Wellington 1974

Phelps, S. *Art and Artefacts of the Pacific, Africa and the Americas* London 1976

Schwimmer, E. *The World of the Maori* Wellington 1966

Scott, D. *Ask that Mountain* Wellington 1969

Scott, D. *Inheritors of a Dream* Wellington 1969

Simmons, D. R. 'A New Zealand Myth' in *New Zealand Journal of History* (3:1) Wellington 1969

Simmons, D. R. 'Economic Change in New Zealand Prehistory' in *Journal of the Polynesian Society* (78:1) Wellington 1969

Trotter, M. and B. McCulloch *Prehistoric Rock Art in New Zealand* Wellington 1971

Vayda, A. P. *Maori Warfare* Wellington 1970

INDEX

ACKNOWLEDGMENTS

David Lewis writes: The main works that have been consulted in preparing this book are listed in the bibliography. However, I would like to acknowledge my special indebtedness to Sir Peter Buck (Te Rangi Hiroa) and Dr. Peter Bellwood. I also wish to thank Teremoana Bellwood of the Te Atiawa Tribe for her help and guidance in steering me past many pitfalls, Tim Curnow for invaluable references and advice, and my wife, Yvonne Liechti for putting up with my consistent preoccupation and for critically reading the manuscript. Special thanks are due to Lisa Myles, a valued collaborator, who coped with my ambiguities and mis-spellings with never-failing patience and good humour.

Werner Forman and the publishers would like to acknowledge the help of the following museums and collections in permitting the photography shown on the pages listed:

Auckland Institute and Museum, Auckland: Title page, 14 above, 26, 30 below, 39 right, 42, 44, 45, 47, 52 below, 58, 62 above, 69, 72, 73, 85, 89, 91 below, 94, 96 above and below, 116, 119; Canterbury Museum, Christchurch: 9, 13 below, 14 left,

24 above, 28 above and below, 83, 91 above, 118; Gavin Gifford Memorial Museum, Te Awamutu: 115; Maori and Pioneer Museum, Okains Bay: Half-title page, 17, 56, 62 below, 80, 124; Museum of Mankind, London: 24 below, 43, 63, 90 right and left, 92, 100, 111, 121 above; Museum für Volkerkunde, Abteilung Südsee, Berlin: 30 above, 37, 39 left; National Museum of New Zealand, Wellington: 8, 19, 22, 29, 46, 52 above, 53, 57, 59, 66, 68, 70, 75, 76, 77, 79 below, 84, 88, 93, 97, 101, 114, 121 below; Private Collection, New York: 98, 99; Taranaki Museum, New Plymouth: 20, 34, 38, 74, 82.

Werner Forman would also like to thank the following museum directors, curators and collectors for their assistance:

Roger Fyfe, New Plymouth; Jill Hamel, Dunedin; E. C. Hunwick, Te Awamutu; Gerd Koch, Berlin; Ron Lambert, New Plymouth; Graham Leech, London; B. McFadgen, Wellington; R. B. O'Rourke, Wellington; G. S. Park, Auckland; David Simmons, Auckland; Dorota Starzecka, London; M. Thacker, Okains Bay; M. Trotter, Christchurch; John C. Wilson, Christchurch; John C. Yaldwyn, Wellington.